Under Pres
Seven plays to re

Paul Francis

Edward Arnold

Contents

Introduction

These plays are about people under pressure – people in fear, facing threats, being tested, arguing about conflicting interests or limited resources. They are primarily intended for pupils at all levels of ability between the ages of 13 and 16, although have both produced and analysed some of the short plays with sixth-formers.

The two longer plays, 'Critical Condition' and 'Facing the Future', can be read around the class, or prepared for performance by a whole teaching group. In addition to being read and studied within normal lessons, they could also be presented to other groups, or to a public audience. There are notes on the production of each play included in the final section, with the suggested assignments.

The five short plays can be used in the same way, or as the basis for group work where small groups work separately on different plays and then present them back to each other, read aloud, acted or recorded (whether on tape or on video).

They also offer an accessible model to teenage writers. The limits of a single setting and small number of characters can be a helpful restraint, and within ten minutes it is still possible to explore important ideas, develop characters, create suspense, tension and atmosphere, or build up to a climax.

As with the earlier collection, *Power Plays*, I have also included some assignments. These ask very different questions in different ways, and will not suit all teachers or all pupils. In other words, they need to be read and thought about before they are set. Many of them imply written tasks which could be done better after or through various forms of discussion, but that decision must be made by the teacher. As always, the best use teachers make of these assignments will be the use that those teachers have chosen for themselves.

P.F

Critical Condition

Jack Read

Eve Read

Sue

Jim

Grandad
(Henry Matthews)

Mr. Gordon Brooke,
*secretary of the Regional
Health Authority*

Members of the Community Health Care Committee:
Mr. Harvey
Miss Millington
Mrs. Phillips

Manor Green Hospital:

Matron

Mr. Roberts,
hospital administrator

Dr. Finch

Sister

Nurse Benson

Nurse Carter

Nurse Stephens

Mr. Collins, *a patient*

Mr. Harry Dodd, *a patient*

Mr. Nicholls, *a patient*

Mr. Webster, *porter and
trade union leader*

Mrs. Grey, *kitchen
supervisor*

Ambulance Man 1

Ambulance Man 2

Porter 1

Porter 2

Jean Moss, *Radio South
interviewer*

Scene One

**Jack Read is having his breakfast, while Eve prepares
breakfast for the children. As she does it she talks,
looking worried.**

Eve: Jack?

Jack: Yes?

Eve: He'll be all right, won't he?

Jack: Who, your dad?

Eve: Yes. He'll be OK, once they get him in.

1

Jack: Oh yes, no problem. He's not keen on hospitals, though, is he?

Eve: Not keen? He hates them.

Jack: Anyway, what are you so worried about? It was your idea.

Eve: That's not fair, Jack.

Jack: Well, it was. You kept going on about how he got on your nerves.

Eve: Well, he did. He still does, come to that. You don't know what it's like, you're out most of the day.

Jack: OK, I'm not arguing. He's your dad.

Eve: That's the trouble. I feel bad about it now, as if I was getting rid of him.

Jack: Well, it's not just you. The doctor says he ought to go in, so by tomorrow night you can stop worrying.

Sue (*entering*): Mum, stop worrying? That'll be the day. (*Sits down.*)

Eve: I wish I could.

Sue: What is it this time? Grandad?

Eve: Yes. Any sign of him yet?

Jack: No chance. It's not lunchtime yet.

Sue: Come off it, dad. he is nearly eighty.

Jack: Trust my teenage daughter to know about being old.

Jim (*entering, in a rush, a bit scruffy*): Breakfast ready yet?

Jack: It's been ready for ten minutes at least.

Eve: And you've still got to clear up your junk from last night. Your grandad goes into hospital tomorrow; at this rate they won't be able to find him, let alone fetch him.

Jim: Why can't we take him in?

Sue: Don't be thick. If he could jump in and out of the car that easily he wouldn't have to go to hospital at all.

Jim: Stretcher job, is it?

Eve: No, they'll probably bring a wheelchair in the ambulance.

Sue: Can we go with him, mum?

Eve: No, Sue, thanks all the same. I'll go. That'll be enough.

Jim: If he knew you'd be there he'd be even more scared.

Sue: Why don't you shut up, little boy? You don't care about anyone else, do you? Will he be in long, mum?

Eve: I don't know. They don't promise. I mean, at his age, anything could happen.

Jim: You mean he might die.

Sue: Sh, don't say that.

Jack: It's got to be faced. It might happen.

Eve: Yes, but it's not likely. It's not as though his condition is critical. Anyway, he'll be better off in hospital.

Sue: That's not what grandad thinks.

Eve: Maybe not, but he's not a doctor.

Sue: But he's still got rights.

Eve: Of course he's got rights, but that doesn't mean he knows best. (*Henry Matthews, Eve's father, enters. He is wearing a dressing gown, and quite enjoys looking a bit different, and complaining. He has heard Eve's last line.*)

Grandad: Who doesn't know best? Talking about me again, are you?

Jim: What are you doing up, grandad? Sue said you could hardly walk.

Sue: No I didn't. I didn't, grandad, honest.

Grandad: It's played me up something rotten, this leg. But I can look after myself, you know. I don't need people running around, ordering me about, talking behind my back. Oh, I'm fed up with it.

(*Jack gets up, having finished a piece of toast, and gulps the last of his coffee.*)

Jack: Here, dad, you sit down here. Give your leg a rest. I'm off. Get some breakfast down you and no more talking.

Sue: But dad, it was you that said –

Jack: No more talking. It's not till tomorrow anyway.

Jim: I'll have a day off school, help carry the stretcher.

Sue: There won't be a stretcher, dummy – unless they need one to get you into school.

Jim: They need a gas mask for you.

Eve: All right, you two. Pack it in. Bye, Jack. (*Jack leaves.*)

Grandad: It's a load of nonsense, if you ask me.

Eve: We didn't.

Sue: That's just it, though. They don't ask you, do they, grandad? They just push you around.

Jim: Yeah, go on, you stick up for him. You could have a march, a demonstration. You and grandad limping down the street – Grandad's Lib rules OK.

Grandad: What's that? What's that, Jimmy?

Eve: Jim, that'll do. Now you get off to school or you'll be late. And you, Sue. I thought you wanted to be at the tech early this week.

Sue: That was the idea.

Grandad: What were you saying, young Jimmy?

Jim: Don't worry, grandad, it was just a joke. You'll be OK, won't you?

Grandad: Course I will.

Sue: Bye, grandad. Take care of yourself. (*Jim and Sue go out.*)

Scene Two

The Community Health Care Committee, which is in charge of running local hospitals. Mr. Harvey, in

3

charge, sits round the table with Miss Millington, Mrs. Phillips, and Mr. Brooke, an important visitor. There are two empty chairs; the Matron and Mr. Roberts wait outside.

Harvey:	Well, we have talked before about the possibility that Manor Green may have to close. I've had a word with Dr. Finch earlier, but now I think we should ask the Matron to come in, and Mr. Roberts, the hospital administrator. (*He gets up.*)
Mrs. Phillips:	It's about time. Someone's got to know what's going on. (*Harvey opens the door, shows Matron and Mr. Roberts in. They sit down.*)
Harvey:	Miss Millington?
Miss Millington:	Manor Green has a very good reputation, and people are happy to work there. It is a small hospital, friendly and caring. On the other hand, small units can be expensive.
Roberts:	You're not saying we waste money?
Miss Millington:	The hospital seems to be efficient –
Roberts:	Seems to be?
Miss Millington:	Is efficient, I'm sure. But the cost of heating, lighting, paying cleaners and so on, does make it expensive. You have the figures in front of you, on the blue sheet of paper.
Harvey:	Thank you. Now we need to save money I'm afraid, in the health service as well as everywhere else.
Mrs. Phillips:	Why? Why not something else? Manor Green costs less than a nuclear missile, or a motorway.
Harvey:	Maybe, Mrs. Phillips. But we are not the government. Of course, if you were Prime Minister . . .
Mrs. Phillips:	Very funny.
Harvey:	This is a Health Service committee, and our job is to look at spending on health.
Mrs. Phillips:	Well, let's spend more, then.
Miss Millington:	Please try to be serious.
Mrs Phillips:	I am serious. People are getting older all the time. They don't die so young, they need more looking after. In twenty years' time we'll need a lot more health care than we do at the moment. More doctors, more nurses, and more hospitals.
Miss Millington:	Maybe, but we don't have unlimited money, and we do depend on support from the government.
Mrs. Phillips:	Huh!
Harvey:	I don't think rudeness will help. We have a visitor today, Mr. Gordon Brooke, from the Regional Health Authority, who is closer to the government and knows more about the whole picture.
Brooke:	Thank you. I know that you're proud of your hospital, and

	I promise you that you're not the only town with this kind of problem. We simply do not have the money to spend on hospitals that we have been spending in the past.
Mrs. Phillips	(*angrily*): Don't we?
Brooke:	No, we don't. You must take my word on that. The sums have been done, and the government has been elected to do what it thinks best. That means saving money, and cutting spending.
Harvey:	And the only way we can save that amount is by closing Manor Green.
Matron:	Close it now?
Roberts:	We knew it was a possibility, but –
Harvey:	That is why we asked you to come to this meeting. We wanted you to be informed by us rather than anyone else.
Brooke	(*worried*): Anyone else? But no-one else knows.
Mrs. Phillips	(*getting up*): But they will do, as soon as I get out of here.
Miss Millington:	Mrs. Phillips, I hope you don't intend to tell the newspapers.
Mrs. Phillips:	That's right, Miss Millington, that's exactly what I'm going to do.
Harvey:	You were invited to a confidential meeting. It will be very hard to trust you in the future if you reveal secret information.
Mrs. Phillips:	What future? You expect me to sit here with this lot going and say nothing? No thanks. I'm elected to stand up for the people out there, and that means telling them what they ought to know. (*She goes out, slamming the door.*)
Matron:	But what is going to happen, exactly?
Harvey:	All doctors and nurses will be able to find other jobs.
Matron:	But the patients –
Harvey:	There are other hospitals.
Matron:	And they're full.
Brooke:	These are difficult times, Matron. We do understand that.
Roberts:	And what do we tell the staff?
Harvey:	Well, they'll have to be ready to move patients, but apart from that say as little as possible. Mrs. Phillips may tell the papers, and in that case we shall have to move fast. I'll come into Manor Green this afternoon. Thank you for coming. (*After a pause, Roberts and Matron realise they are meant to leave. Miss Millington waits until the door is shut.*)
Miss Millington:	What happens now?
Harvey:	We start work, fast. Mrs. Phillips will go to the papers, start a row, demonstrations, that sort of thing.
Brooke:	You have seen the doctors?
Harvey:	Well, I had a word with Dr. Finch. I'm seeing him again this afternoon.
Miss Millington:	What about the other workers – cooks, porters and so on?

Harvey:	I'm talking to their union man, and the kitchen supervisor, but I don't think it's going to be easy.
Brooke	(*collecting his papers*): It's never easy. We simply do what has to be done. Good day. (*He goes out.*)

Scene Three

The men's medical ward in Manor Green hospital. Mr. Dodd, Mr. Nicholls and Mr. Collins are in bed; Mr. Nicholls is grunting faintly.

Collins:	Nurse, nurse. (*Nurse Carter enters.*)
Carter:	What is it, Mr. Collins?
Collins:	My head, nurse. I've got this terrible pain. And he keeps grunting.
Nicholls:	It's my leg.
Carter:	All right, Mr. Nicholls, I'll see to you in a minute. Now, Mr. Collins, what exactly did you want?
Dodd:	Give him a bang on the head, that'll do it.
Carter:	You had your pills at lunchtime, Mr. Collins. You know you can't have any more.
Collins:	But I've got this headache. It's killing me. It's not my fault.
Dodd:	Go on, give the man a glass of whisky.
Carter:	Sorry, we've run out of whisky.
Dodd:	I could just do with a drink. (*Sister enters, worried about the noise.*)
Sister:	Nurse Carter, what is all this noise?
Carter:	Just a headache, sister . . . Mr. Collins is in a bit of pain.
Sister:	Well, what did doctor say?
Carter:	Just the normal dose, sister. Nothing else.
Sister:	That's what he gets, then. A load of schoolboys, you are. Now stop all this nonsense and settle down. (*She goes out.*)
Dodd	(*trying to be funny*): I can't, sister. Whenever I drop off I start dreaming of you.
Carter:	Don't let her hear you say that, or she'll send you home. (*She goes back to the nurses' room, where Nurse Stephens and Nurse Benson are folding laundry.*)
Stephens:	Who was that?
Carter:	Mr. Collins.
Stephens:	Sounded noisy.
Carter:	Well, Mr. Collins had the headache. Mr. Dodd made most of the noise.
Benson:	Mr. Dodd is a headache, if you ask me.
Stephens:	Who, Harry? I think he's a laugh.

6

Benson:	You're welcome. I've too much to do to listen to old men chatting me up.
Stephens:	Don't be rotten. At his age he needs a bit of a laugh.
Benson:	And is that what we're here for? All that training, all this money spent on keeping this place going, just to give a few old fogies a bit of a laugh?
Carter:	He's not that bad. I mean, he's not seriously ill – is he?
Stephens:	Well, he's not going to die this week, but he won't get better, either.
Carter:	Poor old feller.
Stephens:	Just lying there, watching the clock go round.
Benson:	What d'you expect? One kiss from your lovely lips and he's jumping over the beds two at a time?
Stephens:	Don't be silly.
Carter:	No, but it's depressing. When they've got nothing to look forward to.
Benson:	Well, that's men's medical. Little diseases in old bodies. *(Sister enters, looks round.)*
Sister:	Now then, haven't you any work to do?
Stephens	*(standing up)*: Yes, sister. Just finished the towels.
Sister:	Well, now you've got another job. I want as many men as possible ready to move by Friday.
Benson:	What?
Stephens:	But Mr. Collins only came in on Monday. He's not at all well.
Carter:	And Mr. Nicholls isn't ready to go back. He can hardly breathe. He'll collapse if he stands up.
Sister:	Nurse, we have doctors to make the medical decisions, thank you all the same. I'd be grateful if you could confine yourself to carrying out my orders. Is that understood? *(The nurses stand obediently and move off to their work. Sister looks round to check that they're all working, and then goes out.)*

Scene Four

The same day, Tuesday, in the afternoon. Mr. Roberts' office in the hospital. Harvey is sitting in Roberts' chair, and is clearly in charge. Roberts looks worried as he checks through piles of papers, details of the arrangements that will have to be made. There is a knock on the door, after which Matron and Dr. Finch enter.

Harvey:	Ah, Matron, Dr. Finch. Do come in. I've just been going over the arrangements for moving. I think it's fairly straight-

7

	forward. Mr. Roberts?
Roberts:	Well . . . er, yes, I suppose so.
Matron:	There's no way out, then? We've got to move?
Harvey:	I'm afraid so, Matron.
Dr. Finch:	For years we've set a high standard of care at Manor Green, and now that's all wasted.
Harvey:	Oh no. We shall find posts for all the doctors and nurses.
Roberts:	But there is a large number of non-professional staff – porters, cleaners, cooks. What about them?
Harvey:	I have arranged to see them in five minutes' time. Mrs. Grey, the kitchen supervisor, and your porters' union man, Mr. Webster.
Dr. Finch:	So that's it. All over.
Harvey:	Oh no, Dr. Finch. There's a lot to be done. We all have to work to make the transfer of patients and equipment as smooth as possible. I've talked to Mr. Roberts, and he knows what is required.
Dr. Finch:	And when does this start?
Harvey:	Well . . . we ought to start soon, perhaps this week. I have asked Matron to ensure that some patients will be ready for transfer on Friday.
Matron:	But there are some who simply cannot be moved then.
Harvey:	Of course. We must make a start, that is all.
Dr. Finch:	But it is still very sudden.
Harvey:	Swift action, Dr. Finch, but not a sudden decision. We have been considering it for some time. But now we have decided, delay would cause even more suffering than haste.
Dr. Finch:	I don't understand.
Harvey:	There may be opposition to this move – pickets, sit-ins, or demonstrations. Some people may try to prevent movement out of the hospital. If we want to move, we must move fast.
Matron:	What about new admissions?
Harvey:	Very few. And I have authorised Mr. Roberts to phase them out completely in the event of trouble.
Dr. Finch:	I don't know about trouble, but it will certainly cause problems.
Harvey:	Of course. That's why we are warning you in advance, Dr. Finch. I am sure we can rely on you and your colleagues to keep up your high standards of care.
Dr. Finch:	Well, that's all very well, but –
Harvey:	Yes? (*Finch is uncertain, Harvey confident. There is an uneasy pause.*) So that's settled. And now (*looking at watch*) I must be ready to see Mrs. Grey and Mr. Webster. (*Dr. Finch and Matron leave; at the door they almost collide with an angry Mr. Webster, entering, followed by Mrs. Grey.*)

8

Webster:	You'll never do it.
Harvey:	Mr. Webster, we don't need to argue.
Webster:	Right. The argument's over. You're closing Manor Green. Thank you and goodnight.
Mrs. Grey:	Is it definite, then?
Roberts:	I'm afraid so, Mrs. Grey.
Harvey:	It hasn't been announced yet, but it does seem –
Webster:	Certain.
Mrs. Grey:	But what about the staff? Where do we go?
Harvey:	We shall try to save your jobs, Mrs. Grey.
Mrs. Grey:	But where will we work? Most of my ladies come in on the bus. It'd cost them a pound a day to work in the City.
Harvey:	We are aware of the problem, Mrs. Grey.
Webster:	I'll bet my members are more aware of the problem than you are, because they're a lot closer to the dole queue.
Harvey:	There's no need for that, Mr. Webster.
Webster:	Isn't there? Well, I don't suppose it'll bother you too much, you'll be nicely insured. No bother for you having to wait in a queue.
Harvey:	Being rude won't help, Mr. Webster.
Webster:	I tell you this. After this lot, just break your leg and come in on one of our stretchers. You see what happens.
Roberts:	Mr. Webster, there's no need for that.
Webster:	Don't bother. They don't care, none of them. You do realise what this 'll do to the town?
Harvey:	I realise that you have to look after your members.
Mrs. Grey:	That's right, we do.
Harvey:	Just like we have to look after public money.
Webster:	It's not just that. We're providing a service here.
Mrs. Grey:	And it's a good one.
Webster:	And you're killing it stone dead.
Harvey:	Not because I want to, Mr. Webster.
Webster:	Then don't do it. You won't have another chance, you know. Once you close Manor Green and wish you hadn't, it'll be too late to bring it back again.
Harvey:	We've done our sums, Mr. Webster. We just can't pay for it.
Webster:	No? Have you done all the sums? You'll need plenty to pay the compensation that's due. Fuel for moving patients, wasted nursing time, moving the machinery, redundancy money, dole money – it all adds up.
Harvey:	We hope to keep redundancies down as low as possible.
Webster:	Why bother at all, then? I thought you were trying to save money.
Harvey:	We are. It's not an easy decision, Mr. Webster.
Webster:	You'll need my members if you're moving anything out.
Harvey:	And you will need to obey instructions if you're going to be

9

	employed as a porter in this hospital.
Webster:	Who's threatening now? Got that, Mr. Roberts?
Roberts:	Please, I have no wish to be part of this argument.
Webster:	Well, that's too bad. You're in it. Like the rest of us.
Mrs. Grey:	Mr. Harvey, are you sure you can't change your mind?
Harvey:	Nothing would please me more, Mrs. Grey.

Webster: So you keep saying. I hope you mean it. I'm not mucking about, honest. This is a good hospital, and we need it, and the people out there need it. If you had a good look I reckon you'd see that, and all we want is the time for you to think again. But if you do anything in a hurry, you know, make the change before there's a chance of a fuss, well, I'm warning you, there could be real trouble. I mean it. (*Webster goes out, followed by Mrs. Grey. Roberts looks at Harvey.*)

Scene Five

The next morning, Wednesday, in the Read house. Jack Read is gulping breakfast as Jim comes downstairs, followed by Eve.

Jack:	Morning.
Jim:	Hello, dad.
Eve:	What's the rush, Jack?
Jack:	I told you last night. I've got to be in early today. And if Sue wants that lift, she'll have to be quick.
Jim:	She's on her way. Just gone in the bathroom – another couple of hours should do it.
Jack:	Well, she's got five minutes. I'll get my stuff and then I'm off. (*Jack goes out. A brief pause, as Jim gazes into space.*)
Eve:	You awake, Jim?
Jim:	Mmm?
Eve:	Nothing the matter, is there?
Jim:	Mum?
Eve:	Yes.
Jim:	It's today grandad goes in, isn't it?
Eve:	You know it is.
Jim:	He will be OK, won't he?
Eve:	Yes, son, I'm sure he will.
Jim:	Will it hurt?
Eve:	Might do. But it hurts him now. I reckon that's why he gets grumpy. He didn't used to be like that. (*Sue enters from upstairs, without Jim noticing.*)
Jim:	But why does he moan so much?

10

Sue:	Why do you moan so much?
Jim:	I caught it from you.
Sue:	Get lost, peabrain. Mum, shall I get grandad up?
Eve:	No, Sue, don't bother. Thanks all the same.
Sue:	But he goes in today.
Jim:	Are you sure? I thought it was next week.
Sue:	You don't care about anyone, do you? Except yourself.
Eve:	That's not fair, Sue.
Sue:	He's the one that's not fair – selfish brat.
Jim:	I love you too.
Jack	(*looking in briefly. wearing his coat*): Are you coming, Sue?
Sue:	Yes, all right.
Eve:	What about your breakfast?
Sue:	No thanks. My kid brother makes me feel sick. I'll get a coffee when I'm there. You're sure you can manage? I could come home if you want.
Jim:	Yeah, do that. If you're here he'll really want to go.
Sue:	You just don't care, do you? Bye, mum (*Sue follows Jack out. Jim sits, moody. A brief pause.*)
Jim:	I do care, mum. About grandad.
Eve:	I know. but you pretend not to. Why's that?
Jim:	What?
Eve:	When Sue's around, you act as if you didn't care.
Jim:	She just gets on my wick. I mean, grandad can be a pain, moaning on, and going on about how things used to be. But I hope he's all right.
Eve:	They can look after him, love. Go on, get yourself to school, and I'll get grandad ready.
Jim:	Well, I hope it's OK.
Eve:	It will be. We'll fix up for you to visit him – but not with Sue. All right?
Jim:	Yes, I'd like that. See you. (*Jim goes off.*)

Scene Six

The nurses' room next to men's medical, as in Scene Three. Nurses Carter, Benson and Stephens are talking.

Stephens:	But why the hurry?
Benson:	That's not up to us. You know sister, she's in charge.
Stephens:	Yes, and don't we know it.
Carter:	But I mean, old Mr. Nicholls – how's he going to take to being carted over to the City?
Benson:	Nice smooth ride. He won't notice.

11

Stephens:	His wife will. She walks here to visit him. How's she going to manage?
Benson:	God knows. They'll get by somehow.
Carter:	But if they're clearing the patients out –
Benson:	Ssh – they're not supposed to know.
Stephens:	Don't be daft. It's all over the hospital.
	(*Sister enters in time to hear the last comment.*)
Sister:	What is – talking disease? Very catching, that is. Don't want to catch you at it, though, do I? What's the matter, run out of work again?
Benson:	No, sister.
Sister:	Well, let's get on with it, shall we? Nurse Carter, you're the expert on Mr. Collins, aren't you?
Carter:	Well . . .
Sister:	This isn't going to be an easy week for any of us, so I'd be grateful if you could get his pillows fixed – again.
Carter:	Yes, sister. (*Nurse Carter moves into men's ward.*) Now, Mr. Collins, what's the matter?
Collins:	Is it true they're going to move us? I'm in no state to be moved.
Carter:	What do you mean?
Dodd:	They're closing this place down.
Collins:	These pillows are no good.
Carter:	What's the matter, Mr. Collins? Too hard, too soft, too white?
Collins:	I'm not comfortable.
Nicholls	grunts.
Dodd:	Is that right, though, nurse? Are they closing Manor Green?
Carter:	Who told you that?
Dodd:	One of the porters. That young lad with ginger hair.
Carter:	Well, he's bound to know, isn't he? (*Re-arranging Collins' pillow.*) There, Mr. Collins, is that any better?
Collins:	My head aches.
Carter:	Yes, well, we'll do what we can. How about you, Mr. Nicholls? Soon be ready to go home, will you? (*Nicholls grunts.*)
Dodd:	Don't even talk about it. How could we manage without you girls?
Carter:	By then, Mr Dodd, we'll have another lucky customer, and I hope he's not as cheeky as you.
Dodd:	I doubt it.
Carter:	You mean he might be worse?
Dodd:	I mean we won't get another customer, and nor will you.
Carter:	Why not?
Dodd:	That porter said there'd be no more admissions.
Carter:	We'll just have to see, won't we?

Collins:	Nurse, these pillows are all wrong again.
Carter:	All right, Mr. Collins, I'll sort you out in a minute.

Scene Seven

The Read home, later that morning. Eve and Grandad are sitting by the door, waiting.

Grandad:	I told you they wouldn't come. Load of bother over nothing. I reckon I'll get back to bed. (*Knock on the door.*)
Eve:	That'll be them now. Are you ready?
Grandad:	Ready as I'll ever be. This wasn't my idea, you know.
Eve:	So you keep telling me. (*Opens the door, to two ambulance men.*)
A1:	Morning, Mrs. Read. Mr. Matthews, for Manor Green – right?
Eve:	Yes, we weren't sure . . .
A2:	Weren't sure of what?
Eve:	Well, you know. There's been talk of it closing.
A2:	Never. You know us, we never close.
A1:	Well, not today, anyway.
Grandad:	That's a pity.
Eve:	Now, then, dad, don't start.
A2:	What's the matter, Mr. Matthews, don't you fancy a holiday?
Grandad:	I don't fancy hospital. Nasty smells, silly young doctors in white coats prodding you about. I'm too old to be moving around.
A2:	Don't worry, we'll take care of you. Better than Butlin's, we are.
Grandad:	Can I get a drink there, then?
A2:	Oh, we've got a right one here.
A1:	Come on, then, and we'll take you out. (*Carefully, they put Grandad into a wheelchair.*) Are you coming with us, Mrs. Read?
Eve:	Yes, I'll bring his things. OK, dad?
Grandad:	If I was OK I wouldn't be going, would I?
A2:	That's what I say – always look on the bright side. Come on. (*They start to wheel him out, as he moans.*)
Grandad:	I've told them, we don't need all this fuss. They just won't leave you alone. (*They wheel him off, Eve following with a bag of his clothes.*)

Scene Eight

The front main entrance of Manor Green hospital. Most of the action takes place in the courtyard outside the hospital, but people immediately inside the hospital door should be visible. There is a side entrance to the hospital stage right. The scene starts as Mr. Webster and two porters are being shown out of the front door by Mr. Roberts.

Roberts:	I'm sorry, but I shall have to ask you to leave.
Webster:	You will be sorry, and that's a fact. You can't kick us out.
Roberts:	You've been asked to carry out orders, Webster, and you've refused. Clear, reasonable orders.
Webster:	Closing this place isn't reasonable.
Roberts:	That's not for you to decide.
Webster:	Nor for you either. The orders are wrong, and we both know it – so who decides to change them, eh? Someone has to make a stand.
Roberts:	I'm not here to make a stand. I'm here to do my job, and to make sure you do yours. If you won't carry out orders then you're suspended from duty and banned from the hospital.
Webster:	If we can't get in, no-one else can get out.
P:	You can't move patients without porters.
Roberts:	We'll see. (*He closes the door, and stays inside, as Webster and Porters 1 and 2 stand outside, watching. Nurse Stephens comes out of the front door and is in the doorway as Roberts moves to stop her.*)
Stephens:	Mr. Roberts, I need a porter.
Roberts:	They're not working. They're on strike.
P 2:	No we're not. We're shut out.
Stephens:	Mr. Nicholls has fallen out of bed. I need someone to lift him.
P 1:	Right, nurse, we're just coming. (*Moves towards the door.*)
Roberts	(*moving to block the door*): I'm sorry, but I'm not allowing these men back in.
Stephens:	But what's happening?
P 1:	Hitler's running the hospital, that's what's happening.
Stephens:	But why are you shut out?
	(*Nurse Stephens moves outside to talk to them, as Nurse Carter comes to the door from inside, and comes out to join them.*)
Carter:	Look out, Sister's breathing fire. (*To porters*) Is it true you're on strike?
Webster:	Not yet, but we could be. (*Sister arrives at the door.*) You'd better go back.
Sister:	Nurse Stephens, Carter. Come inside immediately.
Stephens:	Yes, sister, but –
Sister:	Now.

Carter:	Sorry, we'll have to go. (*Both nurses go back in, and follow sister back to the ward. Roberts shuts the door carefully. Sound of ambulance arriving.*)
P 2:	What's Roberts playing at?
Webster:	Trying to lock the door, from the look of it.
P 1:	What is this, a hospital or a prison?
	(*Ambulance men 1 and 2 bring on a wheelchair carrying Grandad, followed by Mrs. Read, from stage right. They stop near Webster.*)
Webster:	Hold it, Len. Where are you going?
A 1:	Mr. Matthews, due in to men's medical today.
Webster:	I don't think so. I'd stay there a minute.
Grandad:	Can I go home?
Eve:	No. What's going on?
Webster:	There's a bit of a problem. A dispute.
Eve:	What about?
P 1:	It's not us, it's the hospital.
P 2:	They're closing it.
Eve:	Today? Just like that? They can't do that.
Webster:	You try telling them.
Eve:	All right, I will. (*She goes up to the door, and bangs on it until Roberts opens it, cautiously.*) Now, my father's over eighty and he's been called to this hospital. I've come to bring him in –
Roberts:	Well, I'm sorry –
Eve:	You sent for him. I didn't write this card, you know.
Roberts:	Look, I'm afraid we're having problems with some of the staff . . .
P 2:	You mean you're trying to sack us.
Roberts:	They're refusing to work.
P 1:	We'll take him in.
Webster:	If we all come in.
Roberts:	Will you follow instructions?
Webster:	Depends on the instructions.
Roberts:	You see? It's rebellion. We can't run a hospital like this.
Webster:	If you get what you want, you won't have a hospital to run.
Grandad:	Good. You can drive me home, then.
Eve:	Don't be silly, dad. You're staying here.
A 1:	It's cold enough for us – this old feller must be freezing.
Roberts:	I'm sorry, but my instructions are to exclude these three men. (*Webster takes P 2 aside and points to the side door, stage right.*)
Webster:	Go on, nip in there and get a nurse to take him in. (*P 2 goes.*)
	(*Mrs. Phillips arrives from stage left, with friends and supporters carrying placards 'Let's Save Manor Green' Mrs. Phillips is anxious to make as much of the occasion as possible.*)

15

Mrs. Phillips:	Well, I'm not surprised. That's what you get from cuts: patients dying in the streets.
Grandad:	I'm not dying.
Eve:	I'm just taking him in now.
	(*Jean Moss, a keen young radio reporter, arrives from stage right, holding a microphone. She approaches grandad eagerly*)
Jean:	Jean Moss, Radio South. (*To Eve*) What's the gentleman's name, please?
Eve:	Er . . . Mr. Matthews, Henry Matthews.
Grandad:	Mr. Matthews to you. I can answer for myself, and I'm no gentleman.
Jean	(*(still talking to Eve*): And . . . er . . . how old is he?
Grandad:	Older than you. Now mind your own business.
Jean:	And could you tell me, sir, in your own words, what you think of this situation?
Eve:	Now then, dad.
Grandad:	Don't you 'now then' me. All right, I'll tell you. Cos you want to know I'll tell you what I think of being stuck here on the pavement with a twit of a silly girl asking me silly questions. In my own words, you said. Well, I hope your tape recorder's working because the first words I can think of are why don't you . . .
Jean	(*embarrassed, turning away*): Er . . . well, thanks very much.
Mrs. Phillips	(*moving in, to speak to the microphone*): And the important thing is this – Mr. Matthews is a casualty, just one victim, but it's the whole system which is at fault. Once you start cutting public services people are bound to suffer.
A 2	(*sarcastic*): Vote for me, vote for me. What are you doing about it?
Mrs. Phillips:	I'm Mrs. Phillips. I'm on the Health Committee.
A 2:	I don't care who you are. What are you doing about it?
Mrs. Phillips:	I'm getting as much public attention as I can. We need TV, radio, the newspapers. (*She calls over to a group of supporters, leading them as they chant, aimed at the microphone 'Let's save Manor Green! Let's save Manor Green!' As the chant builds up, Harvey and Dr. Finch arrive.*)
Harvey:	At it again, Mrs. Phillips? Making a noise.
Mrs. Phillips:	Making a noise is better than making a mess.
Harvey:	We'll see. (*He passes through the group to the door, where Roberts lets im in. Dr. Finch is slower to follow, and is approached by Jean Moss.*)
Jean:	Finch, can I ask your view on the closing of Manor Green?
Dr. Finch:	Er . . . no comment. (*He follows Harvey through the door. Porter 2 returns from the side door with Nurse Stephens, and goes to Henry Matthews.*)
Stephens:	We'll take him round the back. He can't stay out here.
Grandad:	I'll go home if you like.

Eve:	No you won't.
Stephens:	Well, if sister catches us –
Eve:	It's been hard enough getting him here. If he doesn't go in now we'll never get him back again.
Stephens:	Fair enough. Now, Mr. Matthews, comfortable?
Grandad:	I'd rather go home.
Eve:	Now then, dad, it's for your own good.
	(*Sister enters, angry, from the side door, stage right.*)
Sister:	Nurse Stephens, I gave you clear orders to stay inside.
Stephens:	Yes, sister, but I had to collect this patient, sister.
Sister:	You had to follow the instructions you were given, unless you wish to be suspended from duty. Now go back inside.
Stephens:	But Mr. Matthews is a new patient. We can't just leave him here.
Sister:	We have no new patients. Mr. Roberts has cancelled all admissions. Follow me this minute.
	(*Nurse Stephens hesitates, and is about to go in, when Matron appears at the front door.*)
Matron:	Sister.
Sister:	Yes, matron?
Matron:	Is this one of our patients?
Grandad:	I feel more like a bloody yo-yo.
Matron:	Bring him in. Come on.
Roberts:	But Matron, I've given clear orders that –
Matron:	Mr. Roberts, our work is to look after people who are ill, and if we can't do that we might as well go home. (*He waits, uncertain.*) I am quite serious. If you don't allow us to bring this patient inside then I am going home. I shall ring the evening paper and tell them that I have been prevented from carrying on my work. The closure of this hospital I can face, but to leave a sick man in the road is madness.
Grandad:	Madness is right, but less of the sick, if you don't mind.
Matron:	Well, Mr. Roberts?
Roberts	(*uncertain, beginning to weaken*): It's a matter of discipline.
Matron:	No it's not. It's a matter of common sense. He comes in, or I go.
Roberts:	Well, matron, if you insist – but just for this case. I can't answer for what will happen later.
Maron:	Someone else can worry about what happens later, and I'm sure they will. Our job, now, is to look after people in need. Ready, Mr. Matthews?
	(*Porters 1 and 2 wheel grandad in, watched by A 1 and 2, and Mrs. Phillips and her group who then go off. The last person left outside is Webster, who is about to go in when Harvey appears at the door, blocking him.*)

Harvey:	All very well, Mr. Webster, but it doesn't solve the problem.
Webster:	Which problem? It's a hospital. Keep it that way.
Harvey:	The money problem, Mr. Webster. We can't afford it.
Webster:	But you could change your mind. Enough trouble, and it could all change – articles in the paper, TV, radio, a couple of horror stories, questions in Parliament. If we got all that, you'd keep it open then, wouldn't you?
Harvey:	I doubt it.
Webster:	I don't. You would for certain. If there was enough fuss. They always find the money if there's enough fuss.
Harvey:	But there won't be. Little hospital, little town, nobody cares.
Webster:	Some of us do. We won today, didn't we?
Harvey:	Today? One day, that's all. When you wake up tomorrow the problems will still be there. No new patients, money being spent that we haven't got. You haven't done a thing. You might as well not have bothered.
Webster:	Don't bother, don't worry, don't care.
Harvey:	We care too, Mr. Webster.
Webster:	Oh, you care. So that means we don't need to. It's all taken care of, none of our business. We might as well be dead.
Harvey:	It's not that bad.
Webster:	Oh yes it is. We're not dead yet, not quite, but it's all going that way. You can't call this a health service; it's sick, very sick, and it's not going to get better. (*He walks off as Harvey goes in and shuts the door.*)

Facing the Future

Ron Marsh	**Jack Riley,**
Barbara Marsh	*a journalist*
Angie	**Kate Furmstone,**
Simon	*a journalist*
Councillor Mrs. Edwards	**Phil Rogers,**
Terry Sharp	a photographer
Maggie Sharp	**Derek Parkin,**
Helen, *Mrs Edwards'*	*the editor*
secretary	**Mrs. Owen,** *headmistress*
Sergeant James	**Tony Harman,** *a teacher*
P.C. Tyler	**Tracy Steel**
W.P.C. Farmer	**Sally Cook**

The play is set in a variety of settings in a present-day English town.

Scene One

The Marsh family having breakfast – Mr., Mrs., Angie and Simon.

Mr. Marsh:	Barbara, I'll be late tonight. Could be any time.
Mrs. Marsh:	What are you doing?
Mr. Marsh:	Some sort of costing exercise. You know, furniture and buildings in a future emergency. I'll get myself something when I get back.
Simon:	Secret government departments today plan to drop a nuclear bomb on Moscow. At his press conference Mr. Ron Marsh, 42, council worker, said –
Angie:	God, Simon, aren't you funny?
Simon:	What's the joke?
Angie:	You, going on about the bomb again.
Simon:	That's no joke.
Mrs. Marsh:	Nor's your dad's job. So stop getting at him.
Simon:	It's the job that's getting at him, not me.
Mr. Marsh:	All right, OK, cease fire. I don't know why I have to keep saying this, but I just work for the council. Is that OK? I thought I was lucky to have a job – am I supposed to feel guilty? Yes, I have to sign the official secrets act, but the only secrets I know are how many tables and chairs there are in this half of the county. Can I go now?

Mrs. Marsh:	There's no need to get narked.
Mr. Marsh:	I feel narked. I'm going, right?
Mrs. Marsh:	You'll leave me the car?
Mr. Marsh:	That's OK, Terry's picking me up at half past.
Mrs. Marsh:	It's nearly that now, and he's always on time.
Mr. Marsh:	Or earlier. Very keen, our Terry. I reckon he's trying to impress Mrs. Edwards.
Simon:	What is it, then, dad?
Mr. Marsh:	What's what?
Simon:	This exercise.
Mr. Marsh:	I don't know. Some sort of future projection thing.
Angie:	Mind your own business.
Simon	(*ignoring her*): You mean you don't know, or can't tell?
Angie:	Stop niggling, won't you?
Mr. Marsh:	I don't need protecting, thanks all the same. I can look after myself. (*Sound of car horn*) There's Terry, honking for promotion. As for you, son, I've got a job to do, and that's how you get fed, so you can lump it.
Mrs. Marsh:	Oh, Ron, before you go –
Mr. Marsh:	Too late, I've gone (*Goes out, slamming doors.*)
Mrs. Marsh:	I'll bet he's taken the keys.
Angie	(*(to Simon)*): You make me sick.
Mrs. Marsh:	Now then, Angie.
Angie:	Well, he does. He keeps going on about the bomb, him and his friends in school. That Tracy Sheldon, always telling everyone what they should think and what they should do. I'm sick of it.
Simon:	Rather have Karen Edwards, would you?
Angie:	Yes, every time. She's a good friend, is Karen.
Simon:	I can't stand her mum.
Angie:	Her mum probably couldn't stand you, if she'd got any sense – and she has.
Mrs. Marsh:	I don't know what you two are on about, but it's time you were off.
Simon:	I just wondered what dad was doing, that's all. Do you know, mum?
Mrs. Marsh:	I wish I did.
Simon:	So you're worried, too.
Angie:	Oh, don't encourage him.
Simon:	You see, it's not just me.
Mrs. Marsh:	It's only since they've started these civil defence preparations. Your dad didn't want to get involved in all that, but –
Simon:	No-one does. That's the point.
Angie:	Go on. Tell us how it all happens.
Simon:	You don't want to know. But some people do.
Angie:	Well, go and talk to them, then.

Simon:	It's only you that doesn't care.
Angie:	Not, it isn't. Mum's fed up with it too.
Mrs. Marsh:	That'll do. It's late, you ought to be off.
Angie:	You don't get out of it that easy.
Simon:	Well, does it matter?
Mrs. Marsh:	I don't know. Of course it matters. I mean, just thinking about bombs that can kill that many people. It's got to matter.
Simon:	You see?
Mrs. Marsh:	But I don't see what we can do.
Angie:	Right. Because there's nothing we can do.
Simon:	Yes there is.
Mrs. Marsh:	What you can do for now is leave me to get on. Go on, I mean it. (*Reluctantly, Angie and Simon go off, as Mrs. Marsh clears up.*)

Scene Two

A office within the government shelter, off the Barkworth Road. The room is small and bare, with two tables and chairs, and perhaps a filing cabinet. Mrs. Edwards enters and looks round. Helen follows.

Mrs. Edwards:	Come along, Helen. The buildings and furniture people will be in here – not a palace but it'll do. Now, there's a couple of phone calls I want you to make but we'll set up first. (*Sergeant James enters.*) Ah, Sergeant James, isn't it?
James:	That's right, Mrs. Edwards.
Mrs. Edwards:	The Inspector has briefed you about this exercise?
James:	Yes, ma'am.
Mrs. Edwards:	I don't want anything clumsy, nothing that'll get in the papers. Just a good efficient job.
James:	I understand. We'll make sure you're not bothered.
Mrs. Edwards:	Nobody comes in, and no-one goes out. Understood? (*James nods.*) Thank you Sergeant. (*James goes, as Ron Marsh and Terry Sharp arrive.*) Come in gentlemen, good morning. I'm glad you're on time.
Mr. Sharp:	Good morning, Mrs. Edwards.
Mr. Marsh:	Morning.
Mrs. Edwards:	I'd just like to go through your part of what we're doing today. The first thing is security. I must ask you to stay here, and have absolutely no contact with the outside world during the exercise – that is vital. You'll go home tonight, of course, and we'll expect you to observe security then, but before then, no contact of any kind. I know it

	sounds a bit silly, but simple mistakes could waste a lot of time and money.
Mr. Sharp:	We understand, Mrs. Edwards.
Mrs. Edwards:	Good. Now, this'll be difficult, but I want you to treat the exercise as if it were the real thing. The figures you'll be getting from the computer may well seem strange, but they are as real as we can make them.
Mr. Sharpe:	Don't worry, Mrs. Edwards. We'll be playing it for real.
Mrs. Edwards	(*not amused*): It may feel like a game, but we have to take it seriously and do it right, so I hope you won't be playing anything at all. Above all, it's not to get to the press. It won't help to have excited reporters sniffing around – there's serious work to be done.
	For today, of course, this is just for the day. With a real attack, we might be here for weeks.
Mr. Sharp:	Excuse me, Mrs. Edwards, but who are 'we' exactly?
Mrs. Edwards:	I don't understand.
Mr. Sharp:	'We'. In a real attack, would we be here alone, or with our families? We do both have children, and –
Mrs. Edwards:	I have children too, Mr. Sharp, and I do understand your concern. Under a nuclear attack, one of the things we want to preserve is family life.
Mr. Sharp:	But –
Mrs. Edwards:	Let me finish, Mr. Sharp. On the other hand, with limited shelter space we obviously can't accommodate everyone. Whether we like it or not, some people are more useful than others, and some families are more important than others.
Mr. Sharp:	Don't get me wrong, Mrs. Edwards. I'm not asking for my family here. I just want to know what the position is. We'll probably do a better job on our own.
Mr. Marsh:	Yes, but some families do come in, and some don't.
Mrs. Edwards:	That's right.
Mr. Marsh:	Who decides?
Mrs. Edwards:	Not me, I'm glad to say.
Mr. Marsh:	But you do know? You know whose family is in and whose isn't.
Mrs. Edwards:	Well, I'm sure I'll be told in good time.
Mr. Sharp:	We don't want your Simon here, Ron, or he'll be signalling to the Russians.
Mr. Marsh:	Is that meant to be funny?
Mr. Sharp:	All right, Ron, don't get narked.
Mrs. Edwards:	As I say, it is not for me to decide. Now, if we can get to the first stage of the exercise, I'd like to begin work on our immediate needs for the first two days. Emergency accommodation, hospital space, that kind of thing. Your office is here. If you could fetch the maps and papers from the van

outside we can get started. (*They go out.*) Helen? (*She comes over.*) I'd like you to ring my daughter's school. I've been told she must be here, so I've arranged for one of the Sergeant's men to pick her up at about eleven. As you'll understand, it's a bit delicate.

Helen: I understand, Mrs. Edwards.

Mrs. Edwards: I know it's not pleasant, but those are my instructions. I'm under orders too.

Helen: It's all right, you don't have to explain.

Mrs. Edwards: Not to you, Helen, maybe. But there are others . . .

(*Helen goes off to ring, as Mrs. Edwards pauses, thinks for a moment, and then goes off in the opposite direction.*)

Scene Three

The headmistress' office in the school. A large desk, with a phone, into which Mrs. Owen is speaking.

Mrs. Owen: Hello . . . yes? Mrs. Owen speaking . . . oh, hello. Nice to hear from you. Is Mrs. Edwards there? . . . I see. Well, do please send her my regards . . . Yes, of course. I'll speak to Karen's teacher at once. Goodbye. (*She holds the receiver, waits for the caller to hang up, then presses a buzzer on the phone and speaks again into the receiver.*) Mary? Could you pop into the staffroom and ask Mr. Harman to see me. Thank you. (*A brief pause, as she thinks about what she'll say, and then looks through a folder of news cuttings. A knock on the door.*) Come in. (*Harman enters. He is a young, energetic teacher, who looks casual without being scruffy.*)

Mr. Harman: You wanted to see me, Mrs. Owen?

Mrs. Owen: Yes, Mr. Harman. Thank you for being so prompt. You're teaching Karen Edwards after break, I believe?

Mr. Harman: Yes?

Mrs. Owen: There's no need to be alarmed.

Mr. Harman: Well, her mother did complain about my teaching, if you remember.

Mrs. Owen (*Looking at the cuttings again*): Indeed I do. I was just looking through the papers again. Still, it's not a complaint this time. Mrs. Edwards has just phoned to confirm that Karen has a dentist's appointment and will need to leave school at half past eleven.

Mr. Harman: Well, I'm glad Mrs. Edwards is happy at last.

Mrs. Owen: I didn't say that, Mr. Harman. She just didn't ring to complain, that's all.

Mr. Harman: She's no reason to. You know what I think of her, and her

23

	council –
Mrs. Owen:	I'm not interested in your political opinions, Mr. Harman. My concern is with your teaching.
Mr. Harman:	My political views don't affect my teaching.
Mrs. Owen:	So I should hope, Mr. Harman.
Mr. Harman:	And they never did.
Mrs. Owen:	Well, that's over now. And I'm pleased to see that you're no longer wearing that provocative badge.
Mr. Harman:	Ban the bomb?
Mrs. Owen:	We don't need to discuss it.
Mr. Harman:	You call that provocative? I suppose you'd be happy if it said 'Buy the bomb'.
Mrs. Owen:	I have never seen a badge with that message.
Mr. Harman:	No. I wonder why not.
Mrs. Owen:	Still, we don't need a political debate. As I say, I'm delighted that you've learnt some discretion –
Mr. Harman:	But Mrs. Owen –
Mrs. Owen:	So if you could remember to remind Karen Edwards about the dentist then I don't think I need keep you any longer. (*Mr. Harman pauses, not wanting to go without saying what he thinks. Mrs. Owen looks at her papers, then looks up.*) Thank you, Mr. Harman. (*Reluctantly, he goes.*)

Scene Four

Maggie Sharp, at home in the kitchen. Barbara Marsh calls on her.

Mrs. Marsh:	Maggie, I'm sorry to drop in –
Mrs. Sharp:	What's up, Barbara?
Mrs. Marsh:	Ron's taken the car keys again, and I wanted to go shopping later on. It's the third time he's left me the car and taken the keys.
Mrs. Sharp:	Well, I wasn't planning on going to the centre today . . .
Mrs. Marsh:	I'm not asking you to take me in. I just wondered – is there a chance you could run me to the offices, so I can pick up the keys? Any time would do.
Mrs. Sharp:	I don't know . . . er . . . I could take you this afternoon. About two. So long as I'm back for the kids at four.
Mrs. Marsh:	That's fine. Ron said he'd be late.
Mrs. Marsh:	So that means Terry will as well. Thanks, that's worth knowing.
Mrs. Marsh:	Didn't he tell you, then?
Mrs. Sharp:	No such luck.
Mrs Marsh:	How d'you mean?

Mrs Sharp:	The past couple of months he's gone all mysterious. Takes his work very seriously, and won't tell anyone anything. I know he wants promotion, and the money would help, but I don't really understand what's going on.
Mrs. Marsh:	What is he doing, exactly?
Mrs. Sharp:	I don't know. I wish I did. Still, there's no point in wondering.
Mrs. Marsh:	Why don't you ask him?
Mrs. Sharp:	He'll tell me if he wants to.
Mrs. Marsh:	It sounds as though he doesn't want to.
Mrs. Sharp:	Well, it's men's work, isn't it?
Mrs. Marsh:	Mrs. Edwards doesn't seem to think so.
Mrs. Sharp:	Oh well, she's different, isn't she? I mean, for a woman to be running the council like that, well . . . it's not normal, is it?
Mrs. Marsh:	I don't know . . . Why not?
Mrs. Sharp:	And your Angie doesn't go in for all these demonstrations, does she?
Mrs. Marsh:	No, but Simon's very keen.
Mrs. Sharp:	That's what I'm saying. It's men's work.
Mrs. Marsh:	Not according to Simon. He keeps saying the bomb is everyone's business. In a way I suppose he's right.
Mrs. Sharp:	Terry wouldn't say so. He's got no time for marches and protests. He wants to be left to get on with his job in peace.
Mrs. Marsh:	Peace?
Mrs. Sharp:	Well, you know what I mean. What about Ron, then? What does he think?
Mrs. Marsh:	I'm not sure what Ron thinks about work at the moment. He's a bit moody, but maybe that's just the kids getting him down. They get at each other a lot.
Mrs. Sharp:	You don't have to tell me. Mine are the same. Except it's only me that seems to bother – I don't think Terry notices. The more that's going on at work, the less he seems to do at home.
Mrs. Marsh:	Yes, well anyway, thanks, Maggie. I'll be round about two. You're sure it's not putting you out?
Mrs. Sharp:	No, that's all right, so long as you're ready. Sorry, d'you want a coffee?
Mrs. Marsh:	No thanks, I'll get back. Thanks, Maggie. (*She goes.*)
Mrs. Sharp:	You're welcome.

Scene Five

The offices of the *Marston Herald*. Kate Furmstone and Jack Riley, both reporters, each have a table,

covered with papers. Phil Rogers, a young photographer, sits at another table sorting various photographs. Derek Parkin, the editor, has come in to speak to Kate; he stands in the middle of the room, reading aloud.

Mr. Parkin: 'When Councillor Bargate rose to speak, at least two of the councillors woke up, and even Mrs. Edwards seemed to be listening with interest.' You don't expect me to print this, do you?

Kate: Why not? You print things a lot duller than that.

Mr. Parkin: Yes, but they're not so rude.

Kate: Do we always have to be polite?

Mr. Parkin: No, if you're writing front pages for the *Daily Mail*, but when you're on the *Marston Herald*, yes.

Kate: What's the difference?

Mr. Parkin: Let me worry about that. Just let me run the paper, because that's my job. Yours is to get stories, and write up the news – not to insult the local councillors. All right?

Kate: I don't agree.

Mr. Parkin: No, but you'll do it. Or get out. What are you covering today?

Kate: Well, there's rumours of a civil defence exercise in one of these secret shelters. Only it's not secret. I thought –

Mr. Parkin: Don't think. Please, please don't think. You can do that in your own time, that and banning the bomb. Save it for the weekend. In our time, and with our money, you get the news. Now (*reading diary*) the Duke of Hereford is opening an extension to the shopping centre at two o'clock, so take young Phil here along with you and come back with a real story. (*Parkin goes out to his office.*)

Kate: Huh. A real story. Duke cuts ribbon, Mrs. Edwards smiles, thousands applaud, flags are waved. Shock, horror.

Jack: That's your trouble, you want excitement.

Kate: And what's wrong with that?

Jack: Life's not exciting, papers aren't exciting. That's what's wrong with it. You'll wear yourself out waiting for it to happen.

Kate: All right, Jack, so what are you waiting for?

Jack: Just the next pay cheque.

Kate: And that's all?

Jack: Pretty well.

Kate: Nothing else?

Jack: Well, there's just one little dream I have, but it won't happen yet.

Kate: What's that?

Jack: Promise you won't tell?

Kate: I promise.

Jack: Well . . . one day I'd like to retire and buy up a brewery.

Kate (*throwing a newspaper at him*): God, you're hopeless.

Phil: You asked for that.

Kate (*to Jack*): You really don't care, do you? If you were me, you'd go, wouldn't you? You'd trot down to the stupid centre, chat up the daft duke about his silly opening and turn out a whole lot of rubbish to fill a few inches on the page.

Jack: That's right. I'd give Parkin what he wants, what he pays me for. What else could I do?

Kate: Look around, sniff around, care. I'm telling you, Jack, there's a story about how this council is preparing for a nuclear war, and you just don't know a thing about it.

Phil: Do you, Kate?

Kate: I know bits. But I'll find more.

Jack: And then what?

Kate: What d'you mean?

Jack: When you've got your story, who's going to print it?

Kate: OK, so Mr. Derek Dumbo Parkin is scared stiff of offending Mrs. Edwards and her posh mates on the platform, but I'm not.

Jack: You know something? You're stupid. They'll spike your story and they'll spike you. Don't you want a job?

Kate: Not any job, Jack. Not at any price.

Jack: Suit yourself. But you're wrong about Mrs. Edwards.

Kate: Go on, tell me. When you get to know her she's a lovely woman.

Jack: I don't mean that. She won't be at the opening. She's sent her apologies.

Kate: Has she now? And I'll bet that's because she's in on this exercise. She's keen on defence, I'll bet she'd fancy a game of soldiers. Hey, Jack, how d'you know?

Jack: That's our job, isn't it?

Kate: All right, clever. But thanks again. Phil, can you do me a favour?

Phil: Yeah, sure. Are we looking for this exercise?

Kate: I am, you're not. You're going to the centre to take nice pictures of the Duke of Hereford and to find out all the exciting things he's doing and saying.

Phil: Well, thanks very much. You want me to go on my own?

Kate: That's right. You're a big lad now. Besides, stories are easier to make up than pictures. You bring the pictures back and some details, I'll write the story later.

Phil: That's a bit risky, isn't it?

Jack: No, not really. Just suicidal.

Kate:	All right, Jack, what are you doing?
Jack:	Me? I'm safe. I'm due in court – which is probably where you'll end up.
Kate:	Yes, well, when it happens I'll give you an exclusive interview. See you. (*Kate goes out.*)

Scene Six

The same room of the shelter as in Scene Two, but Ron Marsh and Terry Sharp have started work. There are papers and maps spread over the tables. They have stopped for a coffee break.

Mr. Marsh:	Well, what do you make of it?
Mr. Sharp:	This'll sound funny, but I'm enjoying it. It's good, this, Ron. Important work.
Mr. Marsh:	But it's hard to take in, isn't it? I mean, thousands burnt, that many hospital beds, contaminated food, all those stray animals . . . Are we going to have all that, really?
Mr. Sharp:	Could be. Anyway, we've got to be ready.
Mr. Marsh:	I suppose so, but –
Mr. Sharp:	No 'buts' about it. We have. There's no argument, Ron – if you can't see that you shouldn't be here.
Mr. Marsh:	No, maybe not.
Mr. Sharp:	I mean it. This job's got to be done, and done properly. That Mrs. Edwards, there's plenty don't like her but she knows what she's about.
Mr. Marsh:	She's efficient, I suppose.
Mr. Sharp:	Got to be. The decisions that are going to have to be taken . . . well, it's no use just guessing. No doubt about it, Ron. She's good.
Mr. Marsh:	Was that girl that came in her daughter?
Mr. Sharp:	Didn't see.
Mr. Marsh:	Just wondered.
Mr. Sharp:	Getting suspicious, are you? You think she's just looking after her own.
Mr. Marsh:	I didn't say that.
Mr. Sharp:	Like she says, it's not her decision. There's got to be some families here, if it's going to go on at all.
Mr. Marsh:	Yes, there's that.
Mr. Sharp:	So why not hers?
Mr. Marsh:	No reason, it's just that –
Mr. Sharp:	There's no point in getting emotional about it. The future, that's what this is about. We've got to think about tomorrow now; if there's going to be a future, if there's

Mr. Marsh:	going to be anything for our kids –
Mr. Marsh:	But our kids aren't here.
Mr. Sharp:	No, Ron, that's not what I meant.
Mr. Marsh:	It's what I mean, though. If this was real –
Mr. Sharp:	It is real. You've got to treat it as real.
Mr. Marsh:	So we never see them again. I walk out on Barbara, Angie, Simon, one morning and that's it. I don't see them again.
Mr. Sharp:	Maybe. That's the risk. It's there, Ron, we didn't invent it. Nobody wants it, but it could happen. (*Helen walks past.*) Helen?
Helen:	Yes?
Mr. Sharp:	Mrs. Edwards' daughter. Er . . .
Helen:	Karen. What about her?
Mr. Sharp:	Is she here, in the shelter?
Helen:	I'm sorry. There's lots of sections. I don't know who's in them all.
Mr. Sharp:	And if you do you're not telling eh?
Helen:	Mrs. Edwards asked if you could be ready to start in five minutes. All right?
Mr. Sharp:	Oh yes . . . Yes, of course.

Scene Seven

A corridor in the school at lunch time. Tracy is talking to Sally, as Simon joins them.

Simon:	They said you were looking for me, Tracy.
Tracy:	Yes, and anyone else. Now listen. There's a full nuclear exercise going on today. Mrs. Councillor Edwards and some of her friends are busy playing cowboys and Indians somewhere down the Barkworth Road – it's only about half an hour's walk.
Simon:	But it's not going to be obvious, is it?
Tracy:	No, and they won't want spectators. They'll have the police out ready, and they won't want us around.
Sally:	So what can we do?
Tracy:	Just because they don't want us, Sal, doesn't mean we can't go.
Sally:	I don't want to start breaking any laws.
Simon:	Just because you're gong out with a copper doesn't mean you can't make a protest. We're not breaking any laws, just saying what we think. Are lots of others going?
Tracy:	I don't know. There's a few talking about it.
Sally:	But what about lessons?
Tracy:	That's the neat bit. It's Thursday afternoon – 'Social

	Responsibility', starring Mr. Tony Harman.
Sally:	But he can't take us.
Tracy:	Of course not. But what could be more socially responsible than making our protest against nuclear war?
Simon:	You could say that, but I don't see Mrs. Owen agreeing with you.
Tracy:	Mrs. Owen doesn't have to know.
Simon:	No, but Harman will.
Sally:	He believes in it. He wears a Ban the Bomb badge, he's bound to let us.
Tracy:	No.
Sally:	What do you mean?
Tracy:	We don't tell him. He can't let us go officially, so if we told him and went he'd get into trouble. He wouldn't want us to ask. We just go and hope he doesn't report us.
Simon:	Yes, that's best.
	(*Angie walks up.*)
Sally:	Just skive off, you mean?
Angie:	Tt tt, the revolutionaries are at it again.
Simon:	All right, Angie.
Angie:	You've not seen Karen, have you?
Tracy:	Yes, she was just asking if she could join.
Angie:	Very funny.
Tracy:	Not to me. Karen's mum may be laughing, but I don't think it's funny.
Sally:	I saw her. Karen, I mean. She went out of History. Had to go to the dentist's, I think.
Angie:	That's funny. She didn't tell me.
Tracy:	I think she got permission from Mrs. Owen instead.
Angie:	Catty, aren't you? All right, sorry I asked. (*She goes.*)
Sally:	There's another thing. When Karen Edwards went out of school I saw Jim pick her up.
Tracy:	What, your Jim?
Sally:	Yes, I'm sure. It wasn't a police car, but it was him.
Simon:	He must be brave – a mere constable chatting up Mrs. Edwards' only daughter. I hope you're jealous.
Sally:	Grow up, Simon.
Tracy:	You'd better ask him. Find out what's going on.
Sally:	Yes, OK. What time are we going this afternoon?
Mr. Harman	(*who has heard the last line, approaching them*): Two o'clock. Social Responsibility. Don't miss your highlight of the week.
Sally:	Yes, well, er . . .
Simon:	How could we?
Tracy:	Where's your badge, sir?
Mr. Harman:	What?
Tracy:	Ban the bomb. You usually wear a badge. What's the

	matter, changed your mind?
Mr. Harman:	I wouldn't say that.
Tracy:	I'll bet Mrs. Owen has been on to you, hasn't she?
Mr. Harman:	Tracy, that'll do. Go on, off to your classes. I'll see you later. (*As they go, Kate Furmstone approaches, in a hurry*)
Kate:	Tony, I've got to talk to you.
Mr. Harman:	What are you doing here?
Kate:	Chasing a story. You know these council shelters Steve told us about?
Mr. Harman:	Yes?
Kate:	Where are they, exactly?
Mr. Harman:	Well, they're dotted about the county. The only one near here is somewhere just off the Barkworth road, across the old railway track.
Kate:	Great.
Mr. Harman:	Why, what's happening?
Kate:	There's some sort of exercise going on. Mrs. Edwards, a few army officers, council workers, police . . . you know the mixture.
Mr. Harman:	And they've forgotten to invite you.
Kate:	Yes, I'll be there. So should you.
Mr. Harman:	I've got lessons to teach.
Kate:	Take the kids there. They'd learn a lot.
Mr. Harman:	Maybe, but I can't.
Kate:	What's up, Tony, losing your nerve?
Mr. Harman:	Don't start preaching at me.
Kate:	Hey, you're usually wearing a badge. What's the matter? After promotion, are you?
Mr. Harman:	I'm not going to get promotion, not after your last little effort.
Kate:	Well, I'm sorry about that, Tony.
Mr. Harman:	'Exciting moves in political education' – you said. That was your story. Well, the only moves I've made since then are down. Mrs. Owen keeps a file of cuttings, and the ones about me she doesn't like at all.
Kate:	OK, I've said I'm sorry. I didn't know he'd cut it like that.
Mr. Harman:	No, but you could guess, Parkin wants to keep in with Mrs. Edwards, you could tell he wouldn't like what I'm doing.
Kate:	All right, call it quits. (*She sees Mrs. Owen come out of her office.*) Watch it – dragon approaching.
Mr. Harman	(*putting on a more official tone of voice*): So if you'd like to contact the Head of History, Miss Furmstone, I'm sure he'll be able to help.
Mrs. Owen	(*coming up to them*): Hello. Are we providing more news for the *Herald* this week?
Kate:	No, Mrs. Owen, it's all right. Just a routine visit. I didn't

	want to disturb you.
Mrs. Owen:	That's quite all right. Besides, Mr. Harman does have a group to register.
Mr. Harman:	Yes, I was just going. (*He leaves.*)
Mrs. Owen:	Well now, can I help you at all?
Kate:	No, thank you all the same, Mrs. Owen. I've got all I need for the moment, thank you. (*Kate goes, watched by Mrs. Owen, who then goes back into her office.*)

Scene Eight

Outside the shelter, off the Barkworth road. Sergeant James and W.P.C. Farmer are standing guard, making sure that no-one goes in through the door, but in fact have nothing to do.

James:	Seems nice and quiet so far.
Farmer:	Yes, it's dead. I don't know why we're here.
James:	That's fine. I hope it stays that way.
Farmer:	It's boring, though, Sarge.
James:	Keeping the peace, that's what we're doing. And nothing happening is peace. (*Tyler comes out from the shelter.*) Get the girl all right, did you?
Tyler:	Yes, no trouble. Funny, though.
Farmer:	That's more than you can say for her mum.
Tyler:	I didn't mean her. All this cloak and dagger stuff. Private car, excuses and that. Why didn't she just come straight here?
James:	Not getting involved, are you?
Tyler:	No, Sarge. Just thinking. Well, I know this girl at the school, see. I was just thinking about it from her point of view. I mean, if she saw Karen Edwards going out – well, it's more of a risk than if she were here from the start.
James:	Tyler, you're not on CID. Save the detective work, eh? You don't have to approve the arrangements, just make sure they work. No-one else comes in, or goes out. It's as simple as that.
Tyler:	And what's going on inside, Sarge?
James:	You just don't ask. It's like council meetings. You keep order outside, and what's going on inside is someone else's problem. I wouldn't even think about it. (*James goes, leaving Tyler and Farmer on duty.*)
Tyler:	You can't help wondering, though. Can you?
Farmer:	I'm beginning to think wondering's a bad idea. (*Mrs. Marsh approaches, a bit flustered.*)

Mrs. Marsh:	Excuse me. I'm looking for Mr. Marsh, Mr. Ron Marsh.
Farmer:	I'm sorry, you can't come in here.
Mrs. Marsh:	He works for the council. Works department, furniture and fittings. It's all right, I've got to be quick – I've a friend waiting in the car.
Farmer:	I'm sorry. You can't come in.
Mrs. Marsh:	It's the keys. He's got the car keys. I need them.
Tyler:	And what makes you think he's in here?
Mrs. Marsh:	They told me, at the council.
Tyler:	Oh, that's great. So much for security.
Mrs. Marsh:	Yes, they said it was supposed to be secret. It's all right, no-one will know. I just want the keys. I mean, they wouldn't tell just anyone, it's just that they recognised me. I'm his wife, Barbara Marsh. Look, I'll wait if you go and ask him for them.
Tyler:	What do you think?
Farmer:	If in doubt, check. You stay here and I'll go and ask the Sergeant. (*She goes, and almost immediately Sally, Tracy and Simon arrive.*)
Sally:	Where are the rest?
Tracy:	I don't know, do I?
Sally:	You said there would be others here.
Tracy:	Well, I thought there would be. It's not my fault.
Sally:	Are you sure this is the right place?
	(*As they get closer to the door, Simon sees Mrs. Marsh.*)
Simon:	What are you doing here, mum?
Mrs. Marsh:	I could ask you the same question. Why aren't you in school?
Tyler:	What's up, Sal?
Sally:	Oh no. Sorry, Jim, I didn't know you'd be here. Honest.
Mrs. Marsh:	What's going on?
Tracy:	Now that is a good question. Well, Jim, Constable Tyler, whoever you are today, just what is going on, eh?
James	(*returning, with W.P.C. Farmer*): What is going on, young lady, is none of your business. From the look of it you'd be better off at school.
Tracy:	Where they can't give us any books because they've spent all the government money on bombs.
James:	Well, that's not up to me. I'm sorry, I'll have to ask you to leave now.
Sally:	Come on, Tracy, let's go.
Tracy:	What are you talking about? What do you think we came for?
Sally:	We've made our point.
Tracy:	We can stay if we like.
	(*Kate Furmstone arrives, in a hurry, with a notebook.*)
James:	If you do stay I am afraid you'll end up in trouble. This is

	council property, and you may be charged with trespass, behaviour likely to lead to a breach of the peace, and obstructing a police officer.
Kate	(*writing notes*): Sorry, sergeant, could you go a bit slower? I didn't get all of that.
James:	I'll give it you in writing, young lady.
Kate:	I'm no lady.
James:	Well, that may be so, but in any case I'll send your editor a copy of any charges. *Marston Herald*, isn't it?
Kate:	And are you making an arrest?
Simon:	No, we're going. Come on, Tracy, let's go.
Tracy:	Don't give in that easily. We haven't started yet.
Simon:	There aren't enough of us. We wouldn't get anywhere.
James:	There will be a full press release from the council offices tomorrow.
Kate:	I can hardly wait.
James:	Sorry, but you'll have to. Come on, please, I'm asking you to move.
Kate:	I could write this up as police harrassment, you know.
James:	You could write it upside down for all I care, love. Just move, eh? (*Simon, Tracy and Sally move away, escorted by W.P.C. Farmer. Mrs. Marsh hangs behind to talk to James.*)
Mrs. Marsh:	Officer?
James:	No, madam, I'm sorry. We're asking everyone to move along.
Mrs. Marsh:	My keys. My husband is in there with the car keys.
James:	I wouldn't know, madam. We can't make exceptions. Sorry.
Mrs. Marsh:	But I've got to have the car –
James:	Sorry, this area's got to be cleared. No unauthorised personnel.
	(*He moves her away, following the others. Ron Marsh comes out from the shelter, followed by P.C. Tyler and Terry Sharp, and is just in time to see Barbara before she goes, although she doesn't see him. Sergeant James returns.*)
Mr. Marsh:	What's happening?
Tyler:	It's all right, sir. Everything is under control.
Mr. Sharp:	Ron, don't be a fool. Get back inside. Let the police look after it. We've got our own work to do.
Mr. Marsh:	But that was Barbara.
James:	It's all right, sir. No problem. They've all gone.
Mr. Marsh:	I can see that.
	(*Mrs. Edwards comes out of the shelter, anxious but businesslike.*)
Mrs. Edwards:	Well, Sergeant, what appears to be the matter?
James:	It's all right, Mrs. Edwards. Handful of demonstrators. Just kids. We've seen 'em off.
Mr. Marsh:	My wife's not a demonstrator.

Mrs. Edwards:	Well, then. Let's get back to work.
	(*She turns to go, and waits by the door.*)
Mr Marsh	(*to James*): But what's happening? What's been going on?
Mr. Sharp:	Leave it, Ron. Come back in.
Mr. Marsh:	No. I want to see Barbara first.
Mr. Sharp:	You can see her tonight. Don't be a fool, man.
Mr. Marsh:	Why, what's the matter? They're not going to shoot me for talking to my wife, are they?
Mrs. Edwards:	Of course not, Mr. Marsh. But we would like to continue with the exercise.
Mr. Sharp:	See? They'll get you, Ron, one way or the other. You've started the job, you've got to see it through, get on with it. This is where your work is.
Mr. Marsh:	Maybe, but I'm not sure I want it . . . I mean . . .
Mr. Sharp:	Don't want a job? You must be crazy? There's thousands of people dying for a job, Ron.
Mr. Marsh:	I don't mean that.
Mr. Sharp:	What do you mean, then?
Mr. Marsh:	Barbara's looking for me. She's my wife, I've got to go, Terry.
Mr. Sharp:	You're out of your mind. You know what the rules are. You've got to stay. You go out now, you'll probably blow the whole thing, secrets act, the lot. the exercise, your job, the whole future. (*He goes in.*)
Mrs. Edwards:	I know it's difficult, Mr. Marsh, but I'm afraid Mr. Sharp is right. We have to think of everyone, not just our own families, The future, for everyone, may depend on a few of us doing our jobs.
Mr. Marsh:	But she's my wife. She's part of the future too. And if this . . . well, if this, here, is the whole future, all there is, well, you can have it. (*He goes off, following Barbara.*)
Mrs. Edwards:	Yes, Mr. Marsh. We probably shall.
	(*Slowly, almost sadly, she goes back into the shelter.*)

Making Sure

Mr. Phelps   **Terry**
Kay Parr   **Gill**
Joanne Richards

Mr. Phelps is showing Joanne round the new office where she is about to start work. It is comfortable and attractive, with plants, expensive furniture and some complicated computer equipment, at which Kay Parr is working – cassette decks, keyboard and VDUs.

Phelps: Now, Miss Richards, we hear good reports of your work in accounts. We're going to move you into the information section, which will give you a lot more responsibility. You'll be working with Miss Parr.

Kay: Hello.

Phelps: You're familiar with this storage system?

Joanne: Yes, I think so. It's like the ones downstairs.

Phelps: But bigger, and better, and faster. When you come to us, Miss Richards, you go up in every sense. Right, Miss Parr?

Kay: Yes, Mr. Phelps.

Phelps: Most of your work will be processing reports. They'll come through by phone or letter, you look up the personal codes, run the programme and get the details off the screen. All right?

Joanne: Yes, I think so.

Kay: You'll soon get the hang of it. It's not difficult.

Phelps: But it is important. Miss Parr will confirm that some of our material here is . . . er . . .

Kay: Sensitive.

Phelps: Exactly. Sensitive. You'll understand what I mean when you've dealt with a few enquiries. In our sort of business we need information on past events, trouble-makers, likely contacts. Anything that might be useful later.

Joanne: Useful to who? Who exactly uses it?

Phelps: It's a government department, Miss Richards. Part of a complex operation. You don't need to know who's on the other end of the phone. If the request gets through, it'll be OK.

Joanne: Sounds simple.

Phelps: It is. Foolproof. You won't get casual enquiries from a call box. We're very careful. Right, I think that's everything –

	oh no. Just one thing. Sometimes, not often but sometimes, we need to erase tapes, wipe them clean.
Joanne:	Oh yes, I've done that. You just replay them, and then press those two while it's running. Don't you?
Phelps:	Not so fast. You're right about the buttons, but you don't use them. Not without my permission.
Joanne:	OK.
Phelps:	This is a very serious matter, Miss Richards. You are responsible to me alone. Is that understood?
Joanne:	Yes, Mr. Phelps.
Phelps:	Good. If you need to summon me in an emergency, just press the buzzer.
Joanne:	Will I need to do that?
Kay:	I'm sure we'll manage, Mr. Phelps.
Phelps:	I will manage, Miss Parr, since this is my department. You will carry out your duties.
Kay:	Yes, Mr. Phelps.
Phelps:	You're confident that you can deal with the work?
Joanne:	I'll do my best, Mr. Phelps.
Phelps:	Good. (*Handing over some files*): There's some long-term requests to be starting on. They're not urgent but they do need to be correct.
Joanne:	Thank you, Mr. Phelps (*He goes. Both Joanne and Kay start work, but slowly, talking as they work.*)
Kay:	What a pain that man is.
Joanne:	He seems to like things exactly right.
Kay:	Oh yes. If there's a paper clip on the floor Mr. Phelps wants it standing to attention.
Joanne:	What's it like here?
Kay:	You've just come up from accounts?
Joanne:	Yes.
Kay:	Well, it's better than that. The money's better, and there's less nagging – except when Phelps is around, of course. Nice and quiet up here, most of the time. They just leave us to get on with it.
Joanne:	It all sounds very secret.
Kay:	Secret's not the word – what's your name, by the way?
Joanne:	Joanne.
Kay:	Hi. I'm Kay. No, you don't call it 'secret' here. 'Sensitive', that's what Phelps likes to call it.
Joanne:	But what's on the tapes?
Kay:	You'll see soon enough. But don't talk about it.
Joanne:	Why not?
Kay:	I'm not kidding. Why d'you think there's a job here?
Joanne:	I don't know.
Kay:	Well, think about it. Comfortable office, fair amount of freedom, responsible job. You'd be daft to leave, wouldn't

	you?
Joanne:	Well, if you put it like that . . .
Kay:	Marie didn't leave. She was slung out. She got nosey one day and ran the programme on a boy she used to go out with.
Joanne:	What was on it?
Kay:	I'm not saying. That's the point. You answer requests. You don't talk about them, and you don't look up things for yourself.
Joanne:	I see.
Kay:	Of course, you can't help getting interested. Just don't talk about it, that's all.
	(*Terry and Gill burst in. Kay reaches for the buzzer but Terry stops her. He points a gun at her head.*)
Terry:	Don't. I'm serious – we've not come all this way for fun. OK Gill, you tell her.
Gill:	You work this machine?
Joanne:	Well, I've only just started . . .
Gill:	Don't play stupid. You work here, you work this machine?
Joanne:	Yes.
Gill:	Right. Then you know it's a nosey Parker machine. Lots of gossip about people your bosses don't like.
Joanne:	I don't know.
Gill:	No, of course. You're just doing a job.
Terry:	We haven't got all day. Get 'em wiped.
Gill:	Alright, don't get mad. Your job, for us, is to wipe the tapes. Just play them through, and wipe them.
Joanne:	What, all of them?
Terry:	Brilliant.
Joanne:	But that would take hours.
Gill:	You'd better start now, then.
Joanne:	I can't.
Terry:	Oh dear. She can't. I'm really sorry for you, darlin'.
Joanne:	But I've been told –
Gill:	And now we're telling you.
Joanne:	Kay –
Terry:	Forget her. You're on your own.
Gill:	Please. We do know what we're doing. We don't want to hurt you.
Terry:	What we're doing is wasting time.
Gill:	Terry, I've got to persuade her.
Terry:	I'll persuade her.
Gill:	Give me a chance, please.
Terry	(*looks at watch*): Alright. Ten minutes. But that's it.
Gill:	Look, my name's Gill McKay.
Joanne:	So?
Gill:	Run my programme now. Go on. The number is 496 28A

GF63.

Kay: How do you know that?

Gill: How did we get in? Your Mr. Phelps isn't as smart as he thinks he is. Go on, run it.

Joanne: OK. (*Nervously, she runs the programme.*)

Gill: Go on, then, read it out. I'm not shy.

Joanne: 'Born Manchester, 11.6.64. Bright school record, college drop-out. Suspected drug offences, seen on anti-bomb marches, Present at riots in Liverpool, South London 1983. Contacts – Michael Healey 721 26B GL 49, Terry Hickling 398 47G FR 61.

Terry: That's me. Autographs later.

Joanne: What's wrong with that?

Gill: What d'you mean, what's wrong?

Joanne: Isn't it true?

Gill: Who cares if it's true? Is there a crime there? Do I get a chance to check it? Do I know who's going to use it? There's bits of me on that tape, and nobody asked me first. I just want them back.

Kay: So you just want your tape wiped?

Terry: Clever.

Gill: No, we want all tapes wiped.

Terry: We're here for other people, not just us.

Kay: All other people?

Terry: Maybe.

Kay: Did they choose you?

Terry: Did they choose you?

Gill (*weary*): OK, what's your name?

Joanne: Who, me?

Gill: Yes, you. Come on.

Joanne: Joanne. Joanne Richards.

Gill (*leaves through index*): Write this down 570 32J LB 26. (*Joanne does so.*) That's your programme. Your very own.

Joanne: But I haven't done anything.

Gill: Don't think that'll save you. Go on, run it.

Joanne: I'm not supposed to.

Terry: I'm not supposed to shoot your friend, but I will.

Gill: He means it. I'm sorry, I couldn't stop him if I tried. Just run the programme.

Kay: Go on, Joanne. You've got to.

Joanne (*bewildered*): OK . . . I don't believe it . . .

Gill (*reading the screen*): There, see. 'Joanne Richards, born Reading 23.9.66. Data operator at information department –'

Joanne: But I've only just got here.

Gill: Ssh. There's more. 'Grandfather active in trade unions, recent drink problems. Brief membership of animal protest movement. Contacts – Mark Rawlings, Borstal 1980, suspected drug offences 1982, possible terrorist leader . . .' That enough for you?

(*Pause, Joanne is stunned, trying to work it out.*)

Joanne: But I went out with him twice. That was all. Two years ago.

Gill: That's enough.

Joanne: I don't understand.

Gill: And you're running it. What chance have the rest of us got?

Terry: Come on, we've wasted enough time as it is. Wipe it.

Joanne: I can't.

Terry: Yes, you can. And you will.

Gill: You do know how to wipe tapes?

Joanne: Yes, but –

Gill: So do it.

Joanne: Let me talk to my boss.

Terry: Oh, that's really good. He's bound to say yes, isn't he?

Gill: You can't ask him.

Terry: We are your boss. (*He shows her the gun.*) As of now, your boss is replaced. Wipe the tapes.

Joanne: But my job –

Terry: Stinks.

Joanne: I need my job.

Gill: Please, just do it.

Kay: Go on, Joanne, you've got to. They'll kill us.

(*Joanne moves slowly towards the machine, then makes a sudden rush and presses the buzzer. She stands, breathless, expecting an attack. The others relax as Phelps comes in.*)

Phelps: Well done, Miss Richards. All right, you two. Thank you. A bit overdone, I thought, but it did the job.

Terry: Cheerio.

Gill: See you. (*They go out casually.*)

Joanne: I don't understand.

Phelps: You don't need to. Let's just say we needed to make sure we could trust you. And we can.

Joanne: So that . . . all that whole thing . . . that was made up?

Phelps: That's right.

Joanne: Just to see what I'd do. That's why they knew the codes. (*Pause*) What if I'd done what they said?

Phelps: You'd have been transferred.

Joanne: What, lose my job?

Phelps: Well, lose this job. You might get another.

Joanne: But . . .

Phelps: Yes?

Joanne: What about . . . no, it's all right. It doesn't matter.

Phelps: Is there something else I ought to know?

Joanne:	No, it's all right.
Phelps:	No it isn't. You were going to tell me that Miss Parr told you to wipe the tapes. Correct?
Joanne:	Well, he did have a gun –
Phelps:	Very loyal, Miss Richards, but you don't need to make excuses. Miss Parr told you to wipe the tapes. True?
Joanne:	Yes.
Phelps:	Well, you should have told me. I'll say it again, you are responsible to me alone. Is that understood?
Joanne:	Yes, Mr. Phelps.
Phelps:	Good. You needn't worry. Miss Parr was acting on my instructions.
Joanne	(*to Kay*): So you knew, all along?
Kay:	That's right. Welcome to the club.
Joanne:	But the tape about me . . . grandad . . .
Phelps:	What about it?
Joanne:	I didn't know anything about it. I mean, it might not be right. Anyone might get hold of it. How can I be sure –
Kay:	You can't.
Phelps:	But we can. I'm sorry, Miss Richards, but we had to make sure. You've done very well, I'm sure you'll be happy here. Good luck. (*He goes.*)

Out of School

Mr. Blakeman	Vikki
Mrs. Blakeman	Craig
Pamela	

The Blakemans' sitting-room. It is comfortable without being luxurious, and if possible should look rather middle-aged and dull. There are a lot of bookshelves, and many of the books look a bit dusty and old – not bright new paperbacks.

Mr. Blakeman:	Well, come on. If we're going, let's go.
Mrs. Blakeman:	And what's that supposed to mean?
Mr. Blakeman:	We're going out, aren't we?
Mrs. Blakeman:	Mark, you agreed that we'd go to see this film two weeks ago.
Mr. Blakeman:	Well, let's get going.
Mrs. Blakeman:	You don't want to go, do you?
Mr. Blakeman:	I didn't say that.
Mrs. Blakeman:	You didn't need to. It's obvious.
Mr. Blakeman:	I just want to go tonight, not tomorrow. That's all.
Mrs. Blakeman:	It's not often we go out. And I did want to see this film.
Mr. Blakeman:	Don't start that again. I've told you, we're going. What more do you want?
Mrs. Blakeman:	The reviews in the papers were very good. You said so yourself.
Mr. Blakeman:	Can we please just get on with it?
Mrs. Blakeman:	All right, I'm ready now. Do you think we'll have to queue?
Mr. Blakeman:	How should I know? It's your idea.
Mrs. Blakeman:	Should we go down and tell Pam we're going?
Mr. Blakeman:	I shouldn't bother. She's in a world of her own, again. I wouldn't think she'd want to see us.
Mrs. Blakeman:	I wish you wouldn't talk like that, Mark.
Mr. Blakeman:	All right, I'm sorry. Now, please, let's go.
Mrs. Blakeman:	Should we leave a light on?
Mr. Blakeman:	No, she'll be OK. She can turn it on herself if she needs it. Come on. (*They turn the light out and go. There is a pause, to suggest that some time has passed. Vikki and Craig enter in darkness, carefully.*)
Vikki:	Come on.
Craig	(*banging into furniture*): Ow. I can't see where I'm going.
Vikki:	This way.
Craig:	What we after, Vik?
Vikki:	Bit of fun, that's all. Now, let's have a look. (*Turns light on.*)

Craig:	What you do that for?
Vikki:	You kept tripping over things.
Craig:	Yeah, but I don't want to get caught.
Vikki:	You know something? You're dead scared. Out in the street you look all hard and that, but in here you're running scared.
Craig:	I'd rather be scared than crazy.
Vikki:	Who are you calling crazy?
Craig:	All right then, Vik, what are we after?
Vikki:	Dunno, do I? Let's have a look first. Might as well take our time. There's no light on, no-one around. Not often you get to see a place like this, eh?
Craig:	So?
Vikki:	Well, come on, Craig, you got to learn. Not everyone lives in a rabbit hutch on Bankside.
Craig:	Knock it off, Vik.
Vikki:	I'm not knocking you. I live there too, you know. I just like to have a look at something different.
Craig:	It's big, isn't it?
Vikki:	Yeah. Look at all those books. Who's going to read all them?
Craig:	Dunno. Maybe he nicked 'em. Hey, can you hear music?
Vikki:	No, darling, but I'm sure we can find you something. I'll just get my violin.
Craig:	No, I mean it. There's a radio, I can hear it.
Vikki:	Only in your head. Cheep, cheep, cheep. Seen anything worth having?
Craig:	No. No ashtrays, fags. Telly's too heavy. Let's go, Vik.
Vikki	(*sitting*): I'm just beginning to feel at home.
Craig:	It's not funny, Vikki.
Vikki:	What's up? Chicken?
Craig:	What are they going to do if they catch us here, eh? Well?
Vikki:	You don't have to worry, Craig. You just do what you want to do . . .
Pamela	(*who has entered quietly, without them seeing her*): Obviously.
Vikki	(*getting up*): Who are you?
Pamela:	Don't mind me. I just live here. Who are you?
Vikki:	We're visiting. Craig, if she makes a run –
Pamela:	Run? Me? You've been watching too much telly. I don't walk if I can help it.
Craig:	Where've you come from?
Pamela:	I am a visitor from the third planet.
Craig:	No, just now. Where were you?
Pamela:	Downstairs. We've got a cellar. Want to see it?
Craig:	Yeah, OK –
Vikki:	No. Stay here. Where we can see you. Sit down.
Pamela	(*sitting*): You sure you don't mind? You know, if I make

	myself at home?
Craig	(*amused*): Hey, that's good.
Vikki:	Shut up, Craig.
Pamela:	What do you want, then? (*Pause*) Just bored, is it? Filling in the odd Tuesday evening with a bit of breaking and entering.
Vikki:	You don't have to act superior, you snotty bitch.
Pamela:	OK, you tell me. What are you doing?
Craig:	It was a mistake –
Vikki:	No it wasn't. We're having a look. Sort of unguided tour, see how the other half lives.
Pamela:	What's your half, then?
Vikki:	Us? That's easy. Bankside estate, Arnold Comp., unemployed. Vandals. That's our half.
Pamela:	Oh.
Vikki:	Heard of us, have you?
Pamela:	Yes.
Vikki:	But it's a bit different here, eh?
Pamela:	Right. Still, I can't help that.
Vikki:	What d'you mean?
Pamela:	Doesn't matter.
Craig:	What were you doing, in the cellar?
Pamela:	Playing a few records. Pretending to work. I've got exams coming up.
Craig:	You still in school, then?
Pamela:	Yes.
Craig:	How old are you?
Pamela:	Seventeen.
Craig:	How did they make you stay?
Pamela:	Couldn't think of anything else. My mum and dad both went to college. I suppose they thought I would. I suppose I will. Sit down – d'you want a coffee? (*She offers to go to make it.*)
Craig	(*sitting*): Great, yeah.
Vikki:	No, hang on. Stay here.
Pamela:	Suit yourself.
Craig:	What's up, Vikki?
Vikki:	Shut up, Craig. (*To Pamela*) What do you think we're going to do, then?
Pamela:	You tell me.
Vikki:	We might slash the furniture up a bit, rip a few books, you know, for a laugh.
Pamela:	Oh yes.
Vikki:	You don't sound bothered.
Pamela:	I'm not.
Vikki:	Let's see. Here, Craig, take a few pages out of one of them. (*She points to the bookshelves.*)

Pamela:	My dad'd go nuts, but it doesn't bother me. For me, you could burn the lot. I'm not kidding. (*Craig goes to the bookshelves, opens a book, leaves through.*)
Vikki:	We'll see. Go on, then, Craig, what's stopping you?
Craig:	Hey, Mark Blakeman.
Vikki:	What?
Craig:	This book, the name in it. It's Fakey Blakeman, used to take us for history.
Vikki:	What?
Craig:	Is that right? Mr. Blakeman, he's your old man?
Pamela:	Yes. 'Fraid so.
Craig:	And he's a teacher at Arnold?
Pamela:	Not just there. He's a teacher all the time, worst luck.
Craig:	Well, get that. (*Puts the book down on a coffee table.*) I didn't know he lived here. 'Course, none of 'em live on the estate, they all drove into work. Car park full of old bangers, bangers full of old geezers.
Vikki:	Well, of course. What do you expect?
Craig:	But we've broken into Fakey's house.
Vikki:	Even better. We'll leave him a message.
Craig:	No.
Vikki:	What d'you mean?
Craig:	I mean no.
Vikki:	Chicken again, are you?
Craig	(*standing*): You can't do everything by calling people chicken. Fakey knows me, he knows I used to go to his school. We do anything here, and they can trace us.
Vikki:	They can trace us anyway.
Craig:	Not if we go now.
Vikki:	She'll shop us.
Craig:	I don't think so.
Vikki:	Well, you're very sure, aren't you? Fancy her, do you?
Craig:	Don't be daft.
Vikki:	It's not me that's daft. She's not for you, Craig. Different league.
Pamela:	Well, thanks.
Vikki:	Don't worry, it's an insult. She's going to shop us anyway, unless we give her a reason not to.
Craig:	What are you getting at?
Pamela:	I'm not making trouble for you, if that's what you mean.
Vikki:	Well, you would say that, wouldn't you?
Pamela:	Maybe. Anyway, it's true.
Craig:	That's right, Vikki.
Vikki:	How do you know?
Pamela	(*standing up, straightening things*): If you don't want a coffee I'd get out before my dad gets back. Before he comes you've got the choice.

Vikki:	Tough all of a sudden, aren't you?
Pamela	(*resigned, sitting down*): All right, have it your own way.
Craig:	She's right. We get out now, we've lost nothing.
Vikki:	And we've got nothing. We've got in here, had the place to ourselves, and done nothing.
Craig:	So what do you want to do?
Vikki:	I want to leave a mark, something that says I've been here.
Pamela:	Here's a pen. You can write 'VICKY WAS HERE' on the wall.
Vikki:	Thanks. I'd rather use this (*She gets out a knife.*)
Craig:	What are you doing?
Vikki:	(*to Pamela*): Who told you my name?
Pamela:	He did. Before.
Vikki:	(*to Craig*): You crumb.
Pamela:	Like you told me his. Craig, isn't it?
Vikki:	So, where'll it be? A nice big V for Vicky, for you to remember me by (*She looks round the room.*)
Craig	(*to Pamela*): You don't care, do you?
Pamela:	Not really.
Craig:	You got all this and you don't care about it.
Pamela:	It's not mine. Not really.
Craig:	You'd rather have it than what I've got.
Pamela:	You wouldn't want this.
Vikki:	No, you're dead right there.
	(*The sound of the front door opening. Craig grabs the knife from Vikki and hides it in a pocket. Mr. and Mrs. Blakeman come in.*)
Pamela	(*rising*): Hello. You're early. What happened?
Mrs. Blakeman:	We couldn't get in. There was a queue and –
Mr. Blakeman:	Pamela, what's going on? (*Looks at Craig*) I know you.
Pamela:	It's Craig, dad. he used to go to Arnold.
Mr. Blakeman:	Yes . . . 5 F, just in front of the back corner. Lindon, isn't it? Craig Lindon.
Craig:	Yes, sir.
Mr. Blakeman:	What are you doing here?
Craig:	Er . . . well . . .
Pamela:	It's all right, dad.
Mr. Blakeman:	I'm not at all sure that it is all right.
Pamela:	Well, let me explain, then.
Mr. Blakeman:	Pamela –
Mrs. Blakeman:	Mark, you should hear what she's got to say.
Pamela:	He's a friend . . . a friend of Vicky's. She's at the college.
Vikki:	What?
Craig:	Yes, that's right. Just dropped in, like. Still, we ought to get off, eh? Come on, Vik.
Vikki:	Yeah . . . OK. (*A bit reluctantly, she follows him out.*)
Mrs. Blakeman	(*after them, too late*): Do stay if you'd like to.

Mr. Blakeman:	Charming friends you've got.
Pamela:	All my friends are charming, dad. You know that. (*She starts to go.*)
Mrs. Blakeman:	Where are you going, Pam?
Pamela:	I haven't finished. I'll just go down and do a bit more on the essay.
Mr. Blakeman:	But we've never seen them here before. If they were your friends why didn't they go down to the cellar?
Pamela	(*going*): Couldn't say.
Mr. Blakeman:	What were they doing? Why did they come?
Pamela	(*as she goes*): Night.
Mr. Blakeman:	Pam never stays in here if she can help it. She didn't tell us they were coming. It doesn't feel right.
Mrs. Blakeman:	I shouldn't worry. She's old enough to look after herself. Sit down, I'll get you some coffee. (*She goes out to make the coffee, as Mr. Blakeman sits down. He notices the book Craig has left on the table, picks it up and starts to leaf through it, worried.*)

Shelter

Mrs. Martin	**Farrell**
Julie	**Stone**
Chris	

A bus shelter on the outskirts of a small town. It's a cold night, with no movement or traffic outside the shelter. Mrs. Martin, a tidy, rather tired looking woman of about 40, sits on the bench, a small suitcase by her feet. She looks at her watch. Julie, aged about 20, runs in, shivering. She is wearing trousers and a short coat.

Julie: Oh, that's a relief. It's freezing out there.

Mrs. M: Mm?

Julie: The last bus hasn't gone, then?

Mrs. M (*sarcastically*): Well, I'm not planning to stay the night here.

Julie: No, of course not. Silly of me. (*A brief pause. Julie looks anxious, trying to be friendly but not wanting to make a fool of herself.*) How long is there to wait?

Mrs. M (*looking again at her watch*): Well, it's due in five minutes, but you never know nowadays.

Julie: That's true. You go into town often, do you?

Mrs. M (*coldly*): As often as I like.

Julie: Oh, sorry. (*There is an uneasy silence. Julie is restless, Mrs. Martin stares straight ahead. Suddenly Chris runs in _ and stops when he sees them. He is about twenty-five, wears jeans and a wrangler jacket, and looks worried, almost wild..*)

Chris: Thank God for that. What time is it?

Mrs. M: I'm not an information desk.

Chris: Oh, stuff it. (*To Julie*) Come on, love, what time is it?

Julie: Sorry, don't know myself.
Should be about five minutes, she says. But she doesn't sound too sure.

Chris (*Offhand and rude, thinking hard*): Thanks for nothing.

Mrs. M: You don't have to blame me. It's not my fault.

Chris: Sorry, I just don't have time to spare. Things on my mind.

Mrs. M: Well, you can tell that to the bus company, not to me.

Julie: Sick, isn't it?

Chris: What?

Julie: Waiting for buses.

Chris: I'm waiting for more than buses.

Julie: What's the matter? Or won't you tell me?

Chris: Well . . . oh, there's no point.

Julie:	Suit yourself.
Chris:	All right, but –
Julie:	Don't tell me you're a bank robber on the run.
Chris:	Not quite.
Julie:	A murderer? Jack the Ripper?
Chris:	Forget it. I knew there was no point.
	(*He walks off a couple of paces, and looks anxiously out.*)
Julie:	No, I'm sorry, I didn't mean to be silly. Can you tell me?
Chris:	Well, I am on the run. In a way.
Julie:	What have you done?
Chris:	Nothing, yet. When's this bloody bus coming? I run this paper, see. Nothing big, just a small newssheet. We write things about government security, that sort of thing – telephone tapping, bugging, secret files.
Mrs. M:	Huh. Trouble-making, more like.
Chris	(*ignoring her*): We've got a piece of news at the moment that's a bit hot. They'd like to stop us printing it.
Julie:	But who's they, exactly? What can they do to you?
Chris:	I can't talk here, it's not safe (*Looking at Mrs. M.*)
Mrs. M:	Don't mind me, I'm sure.
Julie:	But what if the bus comes?
Mrs. M:	It's five minutes late as it is.
Chris:	If it comes, I'll get it. I've got to. At least there's people around.
Julie:	But is that safe?
Chris:	It's safer than walking. And if I'm not in town by tomorrow it's too late anyway. (*Looks again at Mrs. M.*) Come out a minute, I'll explain.
Julie:	Bit nippy, isn't it?
Chris:	This is important. Besides, you might be able to help, later.
Julie:	All right, I'll come. (*Chris goes off, and Julie starts to follow him, as Mrs. M stares.*) No, it's not what you think.
Mrs. M:	Huh. Disgusting. (*A brief pause. Mrs. M looks at her watch again. Farrell and Stone enter. Both are smartly dressed, with warm coats, but Stone is the smarter, and more obviously confident and relaxed. Farrell, a large, muscular man, is clearly impatient.*)
Farrell:	Who are you?
Mrs. M:	I might well ask you the same question.
Farrell:	That's enough lip. Papers?
Mrs. M:	I have my papers, yes.
Farrell:	Give them here.
Mrs. M:	And why should I?
Farrell:	I'm in a hurry, that's why, and I don't have time to hang about. Now will you hand over –
Stone	(*quietly*): Farrell.
Farrell:	Sir?

Stone:	There's no need for the strong-arm stuff. Well, not yet, anyway. We know what we're after and it's not her.
Mrs. M:	I should hope not, indeed.
Stone:	I must apologise for my assistant, madam. Very good at his . . . er . . . side of the job, but inclined to be a touch too eager.
Mrs. M:	Yes . . . er . . . well.
Stone:	In fact, you may even be able to help us with our enquiries.
Mrs. M:	You're police, then?
Farrell:	What's it to you?
Stone:	Not so hasty, Farrell, not so hasty. We are officers, madam, but not the uniformed branch.
Mrs. M:	You've got papers, then?
Farrell:	Who does she think she is?
Stone:	We do indeed have papers, but our authority is classified as top secret. I'm not at liberty to show you my papers.
Mrs. M:	Oh.
Stone:	Of course, if you'd care to call at my office tomorrow morning –
Mrs. M:	No, that's all right, thanks.
Stone:	Good.
Farrell:	We were right on him, we ought to be looking –
Stone:	Now, now, Farrell, in a hurry to freeze, are you? It's cold out there. He'll not be far away.
Farrell:	He'll be further than he was.
Stone:	Farrell?
Farrell:	Sir?
Stone:	I said, he'll not be far away. Do you hear me?
Farrell:	Yes, sir.
Stone:	Don't you trust me, then?
Farrell:	Of course, sir.
Stone:	Well, that's better. We're seeking to interview a young man, madam. A kind of drop-out, you might say, rather scruffy in appearance. About twenty, I should say. (*Julie enters, hearing this. She slows down, trying to look casual.*) Well? (*From behind Farrell and Stone, without them seeing, Julie shakes her head at Mrs. M trying to get her to deny that she's seen Chris.*) We wondered if you'd seen anyone answering that description?
Mrs. M:	Why? What's he done?
Farrell:	We'll worry about that. Have you seen him?
Mrs. M:	I'm not sure . . .
Farrell:	What about this one?
Stone:	One at a time, Farrell, one at a time. Didn't they teach you anything in America? Now, madam, you're not quite sure . . .
Mrs. M:	Yes, there was a boy like that. Rude, he was. Looked

	worried, I'd say. He was talking to her. (*Points at Julie.*)
Julie:	Well, thanks.
Farrell:	Accessory, are you?
Julie:	No, my name's Julie.
Farrell:	Oh, a comic. I like comics. Can we take her back, chief?
Stone:	Farrell, you're getting hasty again. Now, this young man –
Julie:	Chris?
Stone:	Oh, he's changed it again, has he?
Julie:	He's done nothing. He told me.
Stone:	I'm sure that's what he told you, my dear, but I'm afraid it's not true.
Julie:	Really?
Stone:	We need to talk to him.
Julie:	He doesn't seem keen to talk to you.
Mrs. M:	But what's he done?
Julie:	Well, go on, tell her. See, he's done nothing. He's no crook.
Stone	(*to Mrs. M*): I must appeal to your reason, madam. Now, if he hadn't done anything we wouldn't want to talk to him, now would we?
Julie:	I don't know. You might just be after him.
Farrell:	We might just be after you, too.
Julie:	Spite, is it?
Farrell:	Yeah, it's spite.
Stone:	Farrell –
	(*Chris appears, walking slowly away from the shelter.*)
Mrs. M:	There he is, look!
	(*Chris turns to look at them and then slowly joins them, almost as if he's in a dream.*)
Julie:	Chris, why don't you run?
Farrell:	Go on, laddie, run out in the cold. I'd love that. I'll kill him.
Chris:	In front of witnesses?
Stone:	Very wise of you, Mr. er . . .?
Chris:	You know me.
Stone:	I know you. I never know what name you're using, though.
Julie	(*Angry, to Mrs. Martin*): You stupid cow.
Mrs. M:	But he's a criminal.
Chris:	No I'm not. I'm not, am I? Have they told you the charge? Have they? Given you evidence?
Stone:	You're not on trial now.
Chris:	And I'm not going to be, either. You don't work like that.
Stone:	So that's all right.
Chris:	It's all right for you. No publicity, no trouble. Just a gang of cheap crooks in a cellar.
Farrell:	I'll do you.

Stone:	There's no need for it, Farrell.
Chris	(*to Mrs. M*): Don't you see? That's what they are – crooks.
Stone:	You won't, of course, be taken in by this scruffy layabout.
Chris:	Oh, they've got the clothes all right. Very neat. Shown you their papers, have they?
Mrs. M:	Well, we –
Stone:	I don't think you need bother these people.
Julie:	Chris, what can I do?
Farrell:	You do nothing.
Julie:	Chris –
Chris:	Just tell . . .
Julie:	Who?
Farrell:	Go on, son, give her a name. A number. We'll take her round, personal.
Julie:	You'll take me nowhere.
Farrell:	No?
Julie:	Never. You've no right.
Farrell:	Can we take her, chief? Accessory.
Julie:	Accessory nothing. There's no crime, you're not going to charge him, and it's not Chris who's the crook, it's you.
Farrell:	Who are you calling a crook?
	(*As the argument builds, Chris edges slowly towards the edge of the shelter, without making a real move.*)
Ms. M:	Look out, he's going!
	(*Farrell spins round, and rushes to stop Chris. He hardly needs to, Chris stands still, as Farrell grips his arm.*)
Farrell:	Restless, aren't you? Come on, we'll get some exercise walking you back.
Mrs. M:	But what about the bus?
Stone:	There'll be no bus.
Mrs. M:	Well, I know it's sometimes late, but –
Stone:	There'll be no bus. Not tonight. Right, Farrell?
Farrell:	My pleasure. (*He shoves Chris, who starts to move, but stops as Julie comes up.*)
Chris	(*to Julie, almost desperate*): You remember this, right?
Julie:	But Chris –
Farrell:	No, sweetheart, there's nothing. Nothing you can do.
Stone:	I wish you good night. (*Stone bows briefly to Mrs. M, as Farrell and Chris go off, and he then follows them.*)
Julie:	What did you do that for?
Mrs. M:	What do you mean?
Julie:	You shopped him. You gave him away.
Mrs. M:	He didn't seem very bothered.
Julie:	Only because he couldn't get away.
Mrs. M:	Or because he's guilty.
Julie:	How do you know?
Mrs. M:	I didn't trust him.

Julie: Did you trust them?

Mrs. M: They seem to know what they're doing.

Julie: Oh God, is that the best you can think of? 'They seem to know what they're doing.' What are *you* doing?

Mrs. M: Well, I'm not sitting here any longer, and that's sure. If I can't get into town tonight I'll go home and ring Mary. Tell her not to expect me.

Julie: I don't mean that. This – that's just happened. Shouldn't we do something?

Mrs. M: What?

Julie: Well, telephone. I don't think it's right.

Mrs. M: I don't see any problem. It's all under control.

Julie: Yes, but whose control?

Mrs. M: It's no use asking me. Never laid eyes on any of them. (*She picks up her case and walks confidently off. Julie is left watching her. Slowly, she sits down.*)

Chicken

Jackie March   Penny
Scott   Andy Fenton
Dave

Scott and Dave, at a street corner, with nothing to do.

Scott:	Hey Dave, where we going then?
Dave:	Don't know. What d'you reckon?
Scott:	Royal Oak?
Dave:	No. He threw us out last week.
Scott:	That's it. We've got a reason for going.
Dave:	No, let's leave it till Friday, when Barry's here.
Scott:	Any discos on?
Dave:	I don't like discos.
Scott:	Scared of dancing, are you?
Dave:	What d'you mean, scared?
Scott:	Don't get narked.
Dave:	There's no decent girls anyway. (*Jackie walks past.*)
Scott:	It's the indecent ones I fancy. Hey Jackie.
Jackie:	Yeah? Oh, hello Scott.
Scott:	Going nowhere are you?
Jackie:	That's it.
Dave:	You still going out with Andy Fenton?
Jackie:	Very funny.
Scott:	Didn't you hear, Dave? Fenton's moving up a class – right, Jackie?
Jackie:	Toffee-nosed bitch.
Dave:	Who?
Jackie:	Penny 'stuck-up' Harper. God, I hate her.
Scott:	Never mind, Jack, there's better lads than him.
Jackie:	Sure, Scott.
Dave:	He's hard, though.
Scott:	Who, Andy Fenton?
Dave:	Yeah.
Scott:	He's not that hard. We could take him.
Jackie:	You reckon?
Scott:	Sure. What about it, eh Dave?
Dave:	What, just take him on like?
Scott:	What do you want to do, send him a letter?
Dave:	No, but . . .
Jackie:	You don't like Andy do you?
Scott:	No, never have. Nor do you, now.
Jackie:	Well . . .

Scott:	Well? You don't still fancy him, do you? I mean, if he's after that Penny Harper you wouldn't want him, would you?
Jackie:	No . . . no, suppose not.
Scott:	Dave can't stand him.
Dave:	What?
Scott:	Remember that time he said you'd had a brain transplant from a gorilla? (*Laughs.*) Sorry, Dave.
Dave:	Yeah, that's right.
Scott:	So we'll get him, OK?
Dave:	All right.
Scott:	You don't sound too keen.
Dave:	Well, he's not actually done anything to us, has he?
Jackie:	You're not chicken are you Dave?
Dave:	Course not.
Scott:	Right then, we'll look out for him (*Jackie starts to go.*) Where are you going?
Jackie:	Oh, I don't know, get some chips.
Scott:	You fancy a drink on Friday? Royal Oak?
Jackie:	Yes. Thanks, Scott.
Scott:	And let us know if you see Fenton around. We'll be in the chippie later.
Jackie:	Sure, I'll let you know.
Scott:	Come on then Dave, let's have a look at the car park. Pick up a wing mirror or something. (*Dave and Scott go. Jackie is about to leave when Penny approaches from the opposite side, sees her, and tries to move away.*)
Jackie:	Running, are you?
Penny:	No.
Jackie:	What're you doing round here?
Penny:	Is that your business?
Jackie:	You're Penny Harper aren't you?
Penny:	Yes.
Jackie:	I'm Jackie, Jackie March.
Penny:	I know.
Jackie:	That's all you do, isn't it? Just stand there. You make me sick. Do nothing, say nothing.
Penny:	There's not much to say.
Jackie:	You could say you're going out with Andy Fenton.
Penny:	So?
Jackie:	I used to go out with him. (*No reaction.*) You know something, you're a stuck-up bitch. You've got the clothes, nice house, money, so you don't have to do anything. All you have to do is look sweet. You don't live here, you don't belong here; why don't you go home?
Penny:	I'll go home when I want to.
Jackie:	Or when we make you.

Penny:	Who's we?
Jackie:	You'll find out. I'll tell you one thing, you'll wish you hadn't come here tonight.
Penny:	Maybe.
Jackie:	Not maybe. Certain.
	(*Andy approaches, casual, not seeing Jackie at first.*)
Andy:	Sorry I'm late, Penny. Oh . . ., Jackie.
Jackie:	Hullo, Andy.
Andy:	How're you doing?
Jackie:	OK. You know.
Andy:	Where're you going now?
Jackie:	Nowhere special. Just hanging around, getting some chips. I'll see you (*She goes.*)
Andy:	OK.
Penny:	You used to go out with her, didn't you?
Andy:	Well?
Penny:	I just wondered.
Andy:	D'you know her?
Penny:	Not well.
Andy:	She doesn't look your type.
Penny:	No. She's got it in for me since I've been seeing you.
Andy:	No reason. We finished before I went out with you.
Penny:	I wish you'd tell her that.
Andy:	She wouldn't listen. Don't bother about her. That's over.
Penny:	It's over for you. I reckon she still fancies you.
Andy:	Maybe, but I don't fancy her, so that's it.
Penny:	It's alright for you. You're a boy, you can take care of yourself. All the other lads are scared of you.
Andy:	I don't pick fights, not any more.
Penny:	You don't need to. It's different with girls.
Andy:	Yes, my mum told me.
Penny:	No, I'm serious. I mean, I don't think me and Jackie'd ever fight, but I know she hates me. I can see her staring at me, talking to her mates, calling me behind my back. She threatened me just now.
Andy:	You sure?
Penny:	Of course I'm sure. I'm not just making it up.
Andy:	If she's bothering you I'll sort her out.
Penny:	That wouldn't help, Andy. It'd only make things worse.
Andy:	Well, OK then, just forget it.
Penny:	Oh yes, I know. It's just not that easy, that's all.
Andy:	Come on, I'll get you some chips. (*They move away, but are blocked by Scott and Dave.*)
Scott:	Well, guess who it isn't.
Andy:	Hello, Scott.
Dave:	You going to buy some chips then?
Andy:	No, I'm trying to look after your figure.

Dave:	You think you're clever don't you?
Penny:	Come on, Andy, let's go.
Scott:	No, don't go. It's not often we get a classy girl like you around here. What's your name?
Andy:	This is Penny. (*Jackie arrives in the background, eating chips and watching.*)
Penny:	I can talk for myself.
Scott:	You mean you talk as well?
Jackie:	Talk's all you're doing at the moment.
Andy:	What's up, Jackie? Are you still stirring?
Jackie:	Me? No, nothing to do with me.
Andy:	I'll bet.
Jackie:	I'm just a spectator, chewing my chips. You carry on.
Andy:	There's nothing to carry on. Come on, Penny.
Scott:	Penny eh? Cheap, that. Going cheap? Cheap, cheap.
Andy:	Leave it, Scott.
Penny:	Please, Andy, don't worry. I don't mind.
Scott:	Don't you darling? Well, if you don't mind, I don't mind.
Andy:	I said leave it.
Scott:	I've hardly got started yet, Fenton.
Jackie:	You're taking your time.
Andy:	I get it. Thanks, Jackie, thanks for nothing. Come on Penny, let's go.
Jackie:	They're scared. Well, Dave, are you scared?
Dave:	Hold it, Fenton.
Scott:	He's chicken.
Andy:	When I'm scared, Scott, I'll be looking for fights two to one.
Scott:	Well, you've found one, chicken. Besides, there's two of you. cheap, cheap. Chickens going cheap.
Penny:	Very funny.
Scott:	Thought you'd like it. Mind you, she's always been like that.
Penny:	You don't even know me.
Scott:	No, but I could have a lot of fun finding out.
Penny:	I don't think so.
Dave:	You think you're too good for us, don't you?
Andy:	A rubbish van's too good for you.
Scott:	Still, a rubbish van's better than a tramp, eh?
Andy:	What did you say?
Penny:	Andy, come on.
Andy:	What did you say?
Scott:	You're not deaf, Andy, just a little yellow. (*As if giving in, Andy starts to follow Penny, then suddenly turns and rushes at Scott. Scott, shaken by the speed of his attack, shouts to Dave, but is badly hurt. He runs off, chased briefly by Andy, who comes back to face Dave.*)

Jackie:	Careful, Dave, he's mad.
Andy:	You should have thought of that before you started.
Jackie:	It's nothing to do with me.
Andy:	Don't make me laugh. (*To Dave*) Well, you're after a fight, are you?
Jackie:	Go on.
Dave:	Not on my own. No . . . not really. You can stop calling me, though.
Andy:	Yeah, OK. You lay off me and I'll lay off you.
Jackie:	But you said –
Dave:	I said lots of things, but I don't want to fight. (*Turns to go.*)
Jackie:	Chicken.
Dave:	OK, I'm a chicken. What are you? (*Goes.*)
Andy:	Well, Jackie, what are you?
Penny:	You've had your fun, have you? Seen a bit of blood?
Jackie:	It's your blood I'm after. I haven't finished. I'll see you. (*Goes. Andy sits breathless.*)
Penny:	Are you alright, Andy?
Andy:	Yes. Had to be quick. If we'd gone on for long they'd have had me. But I knew he'd be slow. He's big, but he's thick.
Penny:	Cocky, aren't you?
Andy:	Yeah. I'll have to be careful.
Penny:	I didn't want a fight, Andy.
Andy:	Nor did I.
Penny:	No, I know. But if there was one, I'm glad you won.
Andy:	I didn't win. They wanted a fight, I didn't – they got it. Nobody wins. So what the hell are you supposed to do?
Penny:	Oh, that's easy.
Andy:	What?
Penny:	Get some chips. Come on. (*They go off together.*)

Just a Drink

Alan   Denise, *Ben's girlfriend*
Ben, *his friend*   Carol, *Denise's friend*

There are four different settings in this play, and the action should move smoothly from one to the other. It opens at Alan's house. Alan is inside, with nothing to do, when Ben comes confidently to the door. Ben knocks, and Alan opens the door, a bit reluctantly.

Aan: Oh. Hello, Ben.

Ben: Well, come on then, Alan. You are coming?

Alan: Yeah.

Ben: You don't sound too keen.

Alan: No. Well . . .

Ben: Be a good night, this. Don't look so dismal – you look like a corpse.

Alan: I feel like one.

Ben: Well, that's too bad. You'll have to make do with Carol instead.

Alan: Alright. Very funny.

Ben: No, she's alright, Carol. Denise says she's OK.

Alan: You told me.

Ben: Get on great, you will. Don't worry, just leave it to me.

Alan: That's what I wanted to do all along. (*Starts to shut door. Ben sticks his foot in and drags Alan out.*)

Ben: Come on, you don't get out of it that easy. Alan, mate, you can't shiver on the edge for ever. Time to take a plunge.

Alan: I never did like swimming.

Ben: She's good fun, is Carol. Just right for you. (*No reaction.*) Don't you trust me?

Alan: If she's that good, why isn't she going out with you?

Ben: Denise is more my type. Classy, you know. I mean, nothing against Carol, now, it's just that –

Alan: I wish we weren't going.

Ben: You'll love it. Besides, it's just a drink. No sweat, son, we'll be laughing. How can we lose?

Alan: Easy. What's she going to think of me?

Ben: That's her problem. Come on. (*They walk off, to the pub.*)

Carol and Denise, at Denise's house.

Carol: What's he like?

Denise:	Bit of a bigmouth, smooth talker, reckons he's something special. He's all right for a bit of a laugh.
Carol:	Not Ben, I've heard plenty about him. His mate.
Denise:	Oh, Alan.
Carol:	Yes, Alan. The one you're getting for me.
Denise:	It's just a drink, Carol. Bit of a laugh, that's all.
Carol:	Oh yeah. You're setting me up again, aren't you? I've seen it before. Like with that bloke at Christmas. I could have done without him, you know. I'm not desperate.
Denise:	Nobody said you were. I just thought it'd make a change.
Carol:	Go on then, what's he like?
Denise:	Well, Ben says he's a bit shy. You know, just to start. But he'll be alright.
Carol:	Auntie Carol, is it?
Denise:	No. I told you, it's just a drink – you don't have to come if you don't want.
Carol:	Fair enough, I'll come.
Denise:	Mind you, if he's really dishy I'll have him and you can have Ben.
Carol:	Thanks. It wouldn't be the first time. You're not going off him are you?
Denise:	Don't know. Maybe. I just get a bit bored. Same drinks, same pub, same conversation. I'm waiting for something exciting to happen.
Carol:	Where are we going, then?
Denise:	White Swan. Oh, and do us a favour.
Carol:	What?
Denise:	Drink something a bit wilder than tomato juice.
Carol:	I like tomato juice.
Denise:	You won't learn, will you? Come on. (*They go.*)

Alan and Ben, waiting in the pub.

Alan:	Where are they, then?
Ben:	They'll be here. Get 'em in, then. Hey, look at that. Bit of all right, eh?
Alan:	I thought you were going out with Denise.
Ben:	I am. Just like to keep in practice, looking around like. (*Alan passes over drink.*) Cheers.
Alan:	Cheers. D'you reckon they'll turn up, then?
Ben:	Nervous, are you? Don't worry, mate. I'll look after you. (*Denise and Carol enter.*) There you are. Hello, darlin'.
Denise:	Hi. This is Carol.
Ben:	Meet Alan. Denise, Carol. What'll you have?
Denise:	Gin and tonic.
Carol:	Er . . . tomato juice, please.
Ben:	With vodka? OK, love.

Carol:	Um . . . no, thanks, just –
Ben:	You won't recognise yourself. Gin and tonic and a bloody Mary, OK?
Denise:	Told you. (*To Alan*) You keen on bikes too, then?
Alan:	Well, sort of. Haven't got one, though.
Ben	(*returning with drinks*): I might sell him mine when I get a new one.
Denise:	When's that, then?
Ben:	Don't know. Could be soon.
Carol:	What sort of bike have you got?
Ben:	125. But I fancy a bit more power.
Denise:	Don't they all?
Ben:	Well, you were moaning last time you went on mine.
Denise:	I wasn't moaning about the bike. It's the way you ride it.
Ben:	I can always get another passenger.
Denise:	You might have to.
Carol:	Are you going to get a bike?
Alan:	I don't know. Don't think I can afford it.
Denise:	Still at college, are you?
Alan:	Yeah, worst luck.
Carol:	Still, it's better than the dole, eh?
Ben:	I can't wait to get out. Crummy place. I'm sick of being treated like a kid.
Denise:	Perhaps you are a kid.
Ben:	I'm older than you.
Denise:	So?
	(*Uneasy pause.*)
Carol:	My mum says I ought to take some more exams.
Ben:	She's crazy.
Denise:	Are you going to?
Carol:	I don't know. I might. Well, if I'm not going to get a job, I might as well.
Ben:	Get some more loot, more like. They won't pay you to listen to lectures.
Denise:	The way you're going they'll pay you to leave.
Ben:	I can't wait.
Carol:	What'll you do, though?
Ben:	What d'you mean?
Carol:	When you leave college. D'you reckon you'll get a job?
Ben:	Doubt it. Mind you, I wouldn't just take anything. I'd rather be on the dole than sweeping up in a factory.
Denise:	Perhaps they'll make you a manager.
Carol:	What about you, Alan? What'll you do?
Alan:	I don't know.
Denise:	Don't say a lot, do you?
Ben:	Lay off him, will you?
Denise:	What d'you mean? All I said was –

Ben:	I know what you said.
Alan:	D'you want a drink?
Ben:	Now you're talking. Come on, I'll give you a hand.
	(*Alan and Ben take the glasses and move to the bar.*)
Denise:	All right, I'm sorry.
Carol:	Sorry for what?
Denise:	Well, it's hard work, isn't it? He doesn't say a lot.
Carol:	Can't get a word in.
Denise:	Yes. Well, I told you Ben was a bigmouth.
Carol:	You're not doing so badly yourself.
Denise:	Well, he gets me mad. Telling everyone else what's what. Makes me sick.
Carol:	You're not that keen on him, are you?
Denise:	I don't know. I'm just in a lousy mood. Sorry you came?
Carol:	Not yet. See what happens, eh?

At the bar.

Alan:	Gin and tonic, please, and . . . oh, a tomato juice.
Ben:	It was a bloody Mary.
Alan:	She asked for a tomato juice.
Ben:	You're a dead loss, you are. Come on, Alan, you're not saying much.
Alan:	I don't know what to say.
Ben:	Chat her up a bit, make it easier. Just sitting in the corner isn't going to help.
Alan:	It's all right for you.
Ben:	How d'you mean?
Alan:	You just keep rattling on. I can't talk like that.
Ben:	Well, you've got to try. I mean, everyone gets nervous sometimes, but you just have to put on a bit of a show.
Alan:	I don't think I can do that.
Ben:	Well, at least give it a try. Come on. (*Goes back with drinks for the girls. Alan follows with their drinks.*) Where are we going after, then?
Denise:	You paying?
Ben:	Who bought the drinks?
Denise:	Alan, so far as I could see.
Carol:	Is this tomato juice?
Alan:	I . . . I thought that's what you wanted.
Carol:	It was. Thanks.
Ben:	Anyone listening?
Denise:	No, Ben, you're talking to yourself again.
Ben:	I might as well be.
Denise:	You're good at it. Besides, you're the one who really likes to listen.
Ben:	Alright, Denise –
Denise:	You know, I reckon that you're probably your greatest

	fan.
Ben:	You know something?
Denise:	Yes, plenty.
Ben:	Sometimes you're not even funny. See you, Alan (*Goes, angrily.*)
Alan:	Hey, Ben.
Carol	(*to Denise*): Serves you right. You've been pushing him all night.
Denise:	I know. Can't help it sometimes. The mood gets me, and off I go. Or off he goes, in this case. Shall I go after him?
Carol:	Go on, it's your fault.
Denise:	I suppose so. I'll see you. Bye, Alan. (*She goes out.*)
Alan:	Oh, bye.
Carol:	She keeps doing that. Gets boys mad and then tries to make up. I reckon she just likes the excitement.
Alan:	Mmm.
Carol:	What about you?
Alan:	Not me. I don't get excited much.
Carol:	I didn't mean that. What do you do with yourself?
Alan:	Hang around. Play a bit of football. When the weather's decent I go fishing. That's what I really like. Ever tried it?
Carol:	No. Don't know why. No-one ever thinks girls'd fancy fishing. Still, there's no reason why not, when you think about it. I just never did.
Alan:	It's great. Just being there, watching the water. Thinking.
Carol:	Thinking what?
Alan:	Just thinking.
Carol:	You're not keen on bikes, are you?
Alan:	No.
Carol:	I didn't think you were. You know, before, when you said.
Alan:	No, that's Ben. It's fishing I like.
Carol:	D'you always catch something?
Alan:	No. You can spend all day and get nothing, and then you can have a really good day. Last Sunday, that was great – sorry, d'you want another drink?
Carol:	No, I'll tell you what. Drink up and walk home with me, and you can tell me about last Sunday on the way. OK?
Alan:	OK. (*He drinks up, and they go.*)

Assignments

General Notes

Production

Each of these plays can be simply read around the class, but they have all been written in the hope of a more dramatic presentation.

The two longer plays, deliberately using large casts and creating the chance for greater involvement by extras, both need a large floor space. The scenes are short, moving quickly between various settings, so that all that is required is a plan of different areas marked by chairs and tables.

The same applies to the five short plays, although four of them have a single setting and almost continuous action. In a classroom floor space and chairs are sufficient, although for a public presentation it would help to establish the setting more fully – the cold and isolation of 'Shelter', the extensive bookshelves in the Blakeman home ('Out of School'), or the automated luxury of the office in 'Making Sure'.

There is also the possibility that these plays could be used for video, film or radio production. Some specific suggestions are included in the assignments for some of the plays, but there are many other possibilities.

Writing Plays

Some of the assignments in this book ask you to write plays. This can be hard if you haven't done it before, but writing plays can be just as enjoyable as writing stories. It can be funny, or serious, or a mixture; it can help you to think about important ideas; above all, it helps you to think about how different people think and feel.

Don't just start at the beginning of the scene. It helps to think about the people, and what's going to happen, and to write notes on rough paper before you start. If you get a good idea for a speech, argument or action, write that down in rough as well, but don't be in a hurry to start writing in neat.

If you're dealing with a lot of people, you need to sort them into different groups and scenes, and work out how they will come together to tell the story of the play. This was my plan for 'Critical Condition':

1 Family at breakfast – talk about grandad going in.
2 Council offices; committee meeting.
3 Hospital – men in ward; nurses' room.
4 Hospital – Harvey, Roberts plan closure; Webster angry.

5 Next day; Read family at breakfast.
6 Nurses and men's ward – talk about closure.
7 Read home. Ambulance finally arrives.
8 Outside the hospital – porters, Mrs. P, Jean M., grandad . . . Matron; Harvey *v.* Webster.

If a group is working out a play together, it helps to make this kind of plan first, and then to share out the writing of different scenes to different people – so long as they all know what the people are like, and what is supposed to happen. Later, of course, you have to check through the different scenes to make sure that they fit together, but that's useful too.

Writing one scene of a long play is like writing a short play, and that also needs careful planning before you start. This is how my plan looked for 'Chicken' (pp. 54–58)

SETTING: a street corner near a chip shop, rough area	S and D hanging around, chat with J; she sets up quarrel
Andy tough, pleasant, bit cocky, goes out with Penny	J meets P, who's waiting for A Insults, threats
Penny A's girl, quiet, comes from a posher area	A arrives, J goes; A and P talk about J
Jackie A's ex-girlfriend, jealous tough, good at stirring	S and D come back, start row, J comes to watch
Scott Likes to think he's hard, wants to show off, impress J	Fight – S runs, D gives up; J goes, bitter; A and P go off to get chips.
Dave Goes around with S; big, but slow, a bit of a follower	

You need to think about the *people* before you start: not just names, ages and jobs, but what they are like – lazy, attractive, friendly, mean, and so on.

Critical Condition

This is a play with a large cast which in performance needs a number of different acting areas: (a) the Read house, (b) the council office, (c) the nurses' room, next to (d) the men's ward, (e) Mr. Roberts' office and, for the final scene (f) a large space outside the hospital front door.

One way of staging this would be to use a large hall area, with chairs and tables already arranged before the start of the play. The hospital front door could be a line of chalk or coloured tape. The furniture from (a) and (b) could be removed after these scenes, to leave the area (f) completely clear. A plan might look like this:

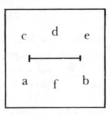

There are lots of other ways of doing it, and it could also be recorded on sound or video, working on the different scenes in different places and then editing them together.

A   Comprehension

1 What differences are there between Jimmy and Sue in the way they talk about their grandad (pages 2–3)?

2 The play shows how different people feel about the hospital being closed. In one sentence for each, describe how the following people feel:

Matron   Dr. Finch   Sister   Mrs. Grey

3 Look at Mr. Harvey and Mr. Webster, especially when they are arguing (pages 9–10). Describe the differences between them, especially dealing with:

each one's attitude to the hospital;
how they feel about jobs, other people, money, each other;
the way they speak (give examples).

B   The Whole Play

1 The title of a play should suggest what it's about, or something important about it. When doctors say someone's in a 'critical condition' they mean they are very ill, possibly about to die. In this play, who or what is in a 'critical condition'?

Grandad (Henry Matthews)   Manor Green hospital
Mr. Williams   all hospitals
one of the patients   something else?

(There may be more than one right answer; it might be easier to talk about it in small groups, to try to agree.)

Then write one sentence of your own, 30 words *or less*, which says what you think the whole play is mainly about.

2 Another clue to what a play is about is the way it ends. This play ends with an argument, in which nobody wins. If the play was performed to an audience, the

66

actors might turn to them – to ask what they think, or to take a vote.

If your class took a vote about the end of the play, would they support Webster or Harvey? What about your family? Most people in the country? When you've thought about these questions, and read through the final argument again (page 18), write three sentences in your own words, beginning:

(a) Mr. Harvey thinks . . .
(b) Mr. Webster thinks . . .
(c) I think . . .

C   The Idea of Pressure

There is general pressure on everyone: the government wants to save money, there is less to spend on hospitals, Manor Green may be closed . . . There are also people under pressure because of this.

In about *five lines* for each, describe the different pressures on each of the following:

Mr. Roberts   Nurse Stephens   Grandad

Mrs. Phillips and Mr. Webster are each trying to apply pressure to change the decision about Manor Green.

What sort of things do they want to use?

How successful do you think they can be?

D   Improvisation

1 In small groups work on scenes within a hospital. For example:

a patient who wants to go home;
a nurse being punished for disobedience;
a rumour that the hospital will close down.

2 This play is serious, and fairly close to real life. Try working out your own scene set in a hospital which is funny, or deliberately exaggerated – an operation, or a silly doctor, or a strange new disease with funny symptoms.

E   Writing

A hospital is a large place with many different groups – nurses, patients, porters, cleaners, doctors and so on. Take another large organisation (a department store, a comprehensive school, a motorway service station, or something else you can think of) and plan out the scenes of a play about different groups who work there. (Read the 'Writing Plays' section on pages 64–65 before you start.)

Facing the Future

In this play, there is a number of small indoor scenes, leading up to an open-air confrontation in a large space. In a large hall it might be staged like this:

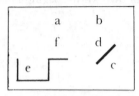

a – the Marsh home
b – the newspaper office
c – the shelter
d – outside the shelter

e – the headmistress' office
f – a corridor in the school,
    perhaps outside (e)

If the play were being presented to an audience, they could either be seated all round the area, or on two sides of it, or in a semi-circle from (b) to (e), passing round (a). The play could also be taped on video or in sound, although it might be necessary to set scenes through sound effects or extra dialogue.

A Characters

1 Simon and Angie argue a lot of the time. Pick *two* things said by *each* of them, to show the differences between them. Then say what you think of each of them.

2 In one sentence (30 words or less) describe the main differences between Jack and Kate in their attitude to their jobs (pages 26–28).

3 In Scene One (page 21) What do you think are Mrs. Marsh's thoughts after the rest of the family have gone out? Write a monologue of about ten lines, giving her thoughts as if you were her. 'They've gone. I . . .'

4 Over the whole play, what main differences have you noticed between Ron Marsh and Terry Sharp? Find as much as you can, and then write a full paragraph (10–15 lines) on each one. Think about:

    their ideas about nuclear war and civil defence;

    their attitudes to their job, and to Mrs. Edwards;

    their relationship with their wives;

    how they behave at the end of the play.

B Ideas

1 In what way is Sergeant James (Scene 5) like Mr. Parkin (Scene 8)? (Clue: *advice* – about what? to whom is it given? what is the advice?)

2 'It's men's work, isn't it.' (page 25.) Mrs. Sharp and Mrs. Marsh don't agree on what is 'men's work' and 'women's work'. In a small group, talk about this list of different jobs, and try to agree on whether you think they are 'men's work', 'women's work' or 'neither' (which might mean that both men and women should do them, or that no-one should, or that it doesn't matter).

68

	men's work	women's work	neither
Deciding to have nuclear weapons			
Deciding to launch nuclear weapons			
Organising shelters and defence			
Running the local council			
Demonstrating against nuclear weapons			
Writing for a newspaper			
Editing a newspaper			
Being head of a school			
Teaching			

Then find as many examples as you can of these things in the play, and make a note of whether they're done by men, or women, or both.

3 How a play ends is important. What does the writer leave you with? What do you make of it?

This play could end in other ways. Instead of the last line, where Mrs. Edwards says 'Yes, Mr. Marsh. We probably shall.' it could be:

(a) Mrs. Edwards: Exactly. We intend to.

or

(b) Mrs. Edwards: Somebody has to.

or

(c) Mr. Marsh: . . . you can have it (*finishing with him, rather than with Mrs. Edwards; in fact, she might have gone in, leaving him alone on the stage*).

Say what you think of each of these, and how they would change the feel of the play at the end. Then say how you think the play ought to end.

4 A lot of this play is about people who are against nuclear weapons, and against spending time and money on preparing for a nuclear war. But not everyone agrees – Angie, Mrs. Edwards, Terry Sharp all think that there ought to be some kind of civil defence, and they don't agree with demonstrations against nuclear weapons. Imagine that you work for Mrs. Edwards, and she asks you to produce an advertising poster, a leaflet and a TV commercial to convince people that it's a good idea to build shelters and prepare for a possible nuclear war.

C   The Idea of Pressure

1 Beneath the general pressure of the nuclear bomb (should we have it? will it be dropped? can we survive?) the play shows pressure building up on various groups of people. Pick *one* of the following groups of people, and describe as fully as you can the pressures on the people in it:

the Marsh family   the newspaper staff   teachers at the school

2 The centre of all these pressures is Ron Marsh. At the end of the play he is forced in different directions, torn between his family and his job. Write 10–15 lines in which you imagine his thoughts as he drives home after leaving the shelter. (If you're stuck, you might start 'I've done it now . . .'.)

D   Improvisation

1 The decision about families in nuclear shelters is difficult. In the play, someone else has made it, and then told Mrs. Edwards (page 23). Imagine that you are a group of officials in charge of shelters. There are only a few people allowed in – people in charge of government, buildings and furniture, hospital services, the police. It's your job to decide:

    (a) if any families should be allowed in, and why;

    (b) how you will choose whose families will be allowed in;

    (c) what you'll do to allow those in but keep others out.

Then try to imagine two more scenes that might happen later, as a result of your decision.

2 In the play, Tracy, Sally and Simon agree not to ask Mr. Harman if they can go to the demonstration. Instead, imagine that they tell him, and that he says they can go. Then work on the following scenes:

    (a) when Simon returns home, after the demonstration;

    (b) Kate gets back to the office with her story;

    (c) Miss Owen and Mr. Harman talk about it the next day.

E   Writing

1 The Bomb is important, but it is hard to write about because it is such a big – and frightening – subject. You might try writing your own scene, perhaps using *one* of these approaches:

    someone who is campaigning against nuclear weapons;

    a group of people deciding whether or not to use the bomb;

    how the bomb affects the way people think and feel;

    after the bomb – what's left?

2 Read through section B3 and 'Writing Plays' on pages 64–65, and then try to write a scene which ends with an important final line. Try using one of these:

'I'm sorry, I wish I could have found another way.'

'Don't you see? It's not just the two of us, it's the end of everything.'

'There's nothing you can do. Nothing at all.'

'This isn't the end, it's only a beginning.'

Making Sure

In a full stage production the set and costumes (of Kay, Joanne and Mr. Phelps) should put across the sense of a comfortable, spacious office, where money has been spent. Costume, too, should underline the difference of Gill and Terry – they will be rougher and harder in their movements, actions and clothes.

The play builds up to a climax, where we understand what is going on, and for an audience that needs to be made completely clear – Phelps is happy, Gill and Terry relax and stop their act, and only Joanne is anxious, trying to work out what is happening and what it means. The audience needs to see all that is happening if they're to understand the play. On stage it can be done all at once; on video you would need to plan the final sequence of shots very carefully; in sound you might have to add some dialogue to make it clear that Gill and Terry were working for Phelps.

Terry has a gun. He needs it to make threats, but how he holds it matters a lot – he isn't a cowboy, and he mustn't just look silly. Would it be any easier if he had a knife? Or a grenade?

A   Character

1 Write a full, detailed character study of Mr. Phelps. Describe:

the sort of person he is;

examples of things he does, how he behaves;

at least two other things people say about him;

at least three different things he says which tell you something about him.

Then, imagining that you are Mr. Phelps, write your report for your boss on Miss Richards' first day in your department.

2 By the end, Joanne has had to do a lot of thinking. She's learnt some things about her job, but she's also had a few surprises, some of them unpleasant. Write 10–15 lines, giving her thoughts as she goes home. You might start 'Well, I'm glad that's over. I . . .'

B   Ideas

1 On page 39, there is an argument between Kay and Terry:
Kay: Did they choose you?
Terry: Did they choose *you*?
In your own words, try to explain clearly what each one means. What do you think about what they say?

2 This play is about storing information, and it gives examples of the different sorts of information about people that a computer might store. Imagine that you are trying to write a law which will say what sort of information the government could store. Your final law must say:

(a)   what sort of information can be stored

(b)   who can see or use it

(c)   how you'd try to make the law work (How could you check? How would you punish people who broke it?)

Some possible suggestions:

(a) date of birth, address, membership of societies, habits and behaviour, details about friends, school report, crimes committed, crimes suspected, medical details, family details, interests, comments from neighbours.

(b) the police, teachers, parents, employers, social security, a friend, the person themselves.

3 Kay is deliberately put under pressure. How? Why? Do you think it is right that Mr. Phelps does this? (Why/why not?) How else could he have found out what he wanted to know?

4 In groups, imagine that you are in charge of training *two* of the following: spy, teacher, bar assistant, TV interviewer, DHSS desk clerk, rock singer, nurse, air pilot, surgeon.

What kind of pressure will they be under? How can you prepare them for that?

C Improvisation and Writing

Work out your own scene in which someone is being tested in some way – perhaps without realising it. Try to keep what's happening a secret until the end of the scene. Possible ideas: a police recruit; an experiment to test people's honesty; an advertisement; someone joining a gang; a new teacher; an actor or actress being tested for a part.

Out of School

The Blakemans' living-room is comfortable, well-furnished and full of books. For a stage version it might be difficult to create this effect, but we should feel that Vikki and Craig are surprised as well as inquisitive; they really haven't seen anything like this before.

A video film of the play could use a real room and real bookshelves, which would help. It might also help to prepare for Pamela's entrance, by including some shots of her working downstairs, intercut with pictures of her parents going out, and with Vikki and Craig when they first break in.

Or would it be better if we *didn't* see her first, so that we are not quite sure who she is? (There is no simple answer to this. It is one good example of differences between stage production and video; different things work differently, you have to think carefully about the choices, and then choose.)

A Character

The play opens with a conversation between Mr. and Mrs. Blakeman (page 42).
   What does it tell you about the two of them?
   How does it help you to understand Pamela?
   How does it prepare for the rest of the play?
   Would it be better if the play started with Craig and Vikki breaking in?
2 Go through the play, finding as many differences as you can between Vikki and Craig. What do they have in common? How are they different? (Think about: breaking-in, their feelings about being there; how they react to Pamela, and what she says; how they behave at the end.)

3 Pamela. Write 10–15 lines about her, which answer the following questions – but not necessarily in order:

What sort of girl is she?

How does she feel about her home, and her parents?

How does she feel about the two who break in?

B Ideas

The threat of the knife is one obvious sort of pressure; what else in this scene puts pressure on Pamela? (Find as much as you can – at least three different things . . .)

What is it like to put pressure on someone else? (Think of a time when you've done it; remember what you did, how you felt at the time, how you think about it now. Make notes, and then go round a small group, each telling your own story in turn – or write it out.)

C Improvisation

In this play, Vikki doesn't use her knife, but she threatens to. Work out your own scene in small groups, using one of the following as a threat, a sign of what *might* happen:

a gun   a brick   a stick   a rope   a paint spray   a box of matches

D Writing

1 Using these characters, try writing one of the following scenes:
either (a) Craig and Vikki walking home
or (b) Mr. and Mrs. Blakeman and Pamela at breakfast next day
2 This scene uses lighting to make some of its effects – Craig and Vikki come in with a torch, and they're scared about putting the lights on. Try writing your own play scene which uses at least one of these: a torch, a TV, the lights of a car, a spotlight, a candle, a cigarette lighter, a camping light.

Shelter

This should be a stage production, because the movement on and off stage would be hard to follow on sound alone, and the audience needs the sense of the shelter there, with a cold, hostile world outside it.

It might be possible to make a video film, particularly of the arguments, but it would need a careful camera script to make the most of the different characters' reactions.

A Setting

Describe, as fully as you can, how this play should be presented on stage. What sort of scenery should there be? (How much? What sort of colours and materials?) What should the lighting be like? What kind of atmosphere should you try to put across? What sort of costumes for each character? (try to find as many clues as you can from the play to back up your answer.)

B Direction

Relationships between people in a play matter a lot, and one way of showing that is where they are – who's sitting and standing, who's close to each other, how far one is from the rest, and so on.

Imagine that the play is being performed 'in the round', with the actors in the middle surrounded completely by the audience. In pencil, work out a diagram which shows where each character would be, and how their positions would change during the play.

C Character

1 What is the relationship between Stone and Farrell? What do they do? How do they put pressure on other people in the play? Is one more powerful than the other? What are the differences between them in the way they talk, behave, do their job, treat each other?

2 In a way, Mrs. Martin and Julie are both spectators, reacting to what they see. Write one paragraph about each one, describing in your own words what they're like and how they feel about what happens. Back up what you say with quotes from the play (at least two for each of them), and find two lines from page 53 which show the difference between them.

3 How much do you know about Chris? Who is he, what has he done, what might he do, what does he want to do, what will happen to him? (You may have to guess the answers to some of these, but use the play to help you as far as you can.)

D Improvisation or Writing

1 In a way, the end of the play doesn't finish the story.
Either (a) Work out your own ending, which you think would work well, coming after the play as it is – or changing some of it.
Or (b) Make up a scene which carries the story on:
    (i) Julie getting in touch with Chris's friends;
    (ii) Farrell and Stone interrogating Chris;
    (iii) Mrs. Martin getting home and hearing more news about Chris.

2 This play makes use of a particular setting – it would be very different in a crowded bus station, or at noon on a hot day in August. Work out a scene which makes use of one of these settings: an oasis in the desert; a hut during a storm; a cave; a lift; a tent.

74

Chicken

The first group who did this play painted a graffiti wall as a background, and at one time suggested making a video of it outside the local chip shop, but that would have been difficult. There are different ways of presenting the play, but all it really needs is some space and five people.

The positioning is important. There must be a clear idea of where the chip shop is, of how Dave and Scott block Andy – they literally leave him no way out. And with the fight, the spacing has to be exactly right, for Andy to convince us that he could deal with Scott without Dave having time to join in.

Then there is Jackie. 'I'm just a spectator', she says, but she's a lot more than that. Where she stands, and how she stands, could make a lot of difference.

A Character

1 Andy doesn't want a fight, but he ends up with one. Could he have avoided it? Is the fight in any way his fault? If so, how? Write 10–15 lines about the sort of person he is, and the full reasons why the fight started.

2 Jackie used to go out with Andy, and Penny does now. What other differences are there between them? What do you think of each one? Do you like one more than the other?

3 Andy, the centre of the play, is obviously under pressure. But so are each of the other characters, in different ways. Write one sentence for each character, describing the different ways in which they are under pressure. (Clues: what do they want? what do they fear?)

B Ideas

1 Penny says 'It's different with girls.' She's talking about rows and arguments, and thinks there is a difference between the way girls disagree and the way boys disagree.

Is she right? Are there differences between the sexes in the way they quarrel? Do girls fight each other? Should they? Why/why not? Think of examples – people and arguments that you've known.

2 Why is this play called 'Chicken'? What does the idea of being called 'chicken' mean –

to Andy?	to Dave?	to Jackie?

What sort of things are people called 'chicken' for? Would it worry you to be called 'chicken'? (Try to think of examples.) Would you call someone else 'chicken'? (Why?) Does it matter?

Write about 15 lines of your thoughts about these questions, but you don't have to deal with all of them, or do them in order. If you think of other things to say apart from the questions, add those as well.

C Improvisation

In a group of six or less work out a scene which takes place in the Royal Oak the next Friday. You must include Dave, Scott and Jackie, but can also use Penny and Andy if you want. Try it a number of different ways to see what works best.

D Writing

Using the characters from this play, write a scene which takes place later:

Either   (a)   when Dave and Scott meet again. (How has Dave changed since the start of the play?)

Or   (b)   the next time Jackie and Penny meet.

Just a Drink

This is the only one of the short plays to move between different settings. It is no necessary to have scenery for this play, and it would get in the way to have a pub ful of people who have nothing to say. What matters is the four main people and wha they say to each other, so doors, drinks, bar staff and streets can all be imaginary.

For that reason this is probably the play which is best suited to a radio production There are only four different voices to get to know and the characters are each very different from each other. What sound effects could you use to help set the scene (Make a list – there are quite a few possibilities . . .)

A Character

1 'What's she going to think of me?' Alan is worried about what Carol will think o him. By the end of the play, what would she say about him? Write 5–10 lines of wha she might say to Denise later.

2 Denise says to Ben 'Perhaps they'll make you a manager.' (p. 61.) What does she mean? What is she trying to say about Ben? Look at what he says about jobs, and then say if you agree with Ben or Denise, and why.

3 From the list below, try to find at least *two* different words which fit *each* of the characters in the play:

shy   nervous   terrified   confident   big-headed   selfish   generous   honest
lazy   friendly   two-faced   nasty   rude   sarcastic   witty   moody   well-meaning
cruel   intelligent   stupid   interesting   interested   helpful   thoughtless
self-centred   ambitious   inconsiderate   lonely

If you want, add more ideas of your own.

B Ideas

1 'Time to take a plunge . . . You just have to put on a bit of a show.' Ben has clea ideas about how you should behave when you're out with someone for the first time Is he right? Does he help? (Find examples of what different people say; pick out the ones that you think help people to get on together, and the ones which make thing: worse.)

2 In groups (both sexes, five or less) work out your own list of 'Ten Rules for Going Out' – things to do, things not to do. You should think about: asking out in the firs place; ordering food or drinks; paying for them; deciding what to do next; making conversation; and anything else you think is important.

C Writing

1 Plan your own play scene about four people, two boys and two girls. Have a clear idea about each person before you start, and find at least *two* different character words for each one. (Use the list in A 3 to help if you want, but add other words as well.)

When you come to write the scene, you don't have to have all four people there at the same time. 'Just a Drink' splits them up a bit – the journey to the pub, buying drinks at the bar, Ben going off in a temper, and so on.

When a number of scenes have been written, you need to try them out by reading them or acting them out, and then talk about how they worked, and how you could make them better.

2 Alan is under pressure, because he hasn't got a girlfriend, is shy about talking to girls he doesn't know, and isn't sure how to behave. In this scene, he's lucky because Carol wants to talk to him and helps him to feel more confident. Imagine that he takes her home and then walks home alone. Write ten lines describing his thoughts. (If you get stuck, you might start. 'She's nice. I didn't think . . .')

3 Sometimes people who know each other well try to put each other under pressure. How do Ben and Denise make things difficult for each other? (Make a list – as many things as you can find.)

Why do you think they do this?

Pressure: Further Work

A pressure cooker shuts the steam in to cook the food faster; tyre pressure is the air that's forced in to keep the tyre hard; a pressure group is made of peole who want to make the government do something. People 'under pressure' are being forced – they are being made to do something, or stopped from doing something, and that puts a strain on them. These plays are about pressure of different kinds, and when you've read a lot of them it's worth thinking about that central idea.

Some suggestions to work on:

1 Write an essay called 'People Under Pressure'. You should include at least four of the characters in this book, each from a different play – describe them and what they do, and use quotes (by them, to them, or about them); then say what you think of them – do you like them, or feel sorry for them? Would you do what they did? Then say something about who or what puts them under pressure; are they under the same sorts of pressure as each other – or different?

The plan for your essay might look like this:

Why you picked each of the four people

Four character studies (description, examples, quotes, comment)

How are they different? How are they the same?

What kinds of pressure are they under?

Your thoughts about pressure, and what it does to people in these plays

2 Most of the pressures in these plays are threatening or frightening. Are there ways in which pressure can be a good thing, which brings out the best in people, or teaches them something new?

Make a list of examples, of *five* good kinds of pressure. Then plan out a play scene about one of them (no more than five people, no more than ten minutes long).

3 Think about a time when you were 'under pressure'. What happened? What was it like? How did you feel? How do you feel about it now, looking back? (You might tell each other your own stories in small groups, to see what different people remember.)

Then try turning that into *either* a story *or* a play. Think carefully first which one you'll do, and why, and write ten lines on

'Why I'd rather write a story . . .'

'Why I'd rather write a play . . .'

– and then write it!

4 Some of the pressures in these plays are general pressures, ones that lots of people feel – government cuts in money for hospitals, the fear of the nuclear bomb. Try to think of *four* general pressures, one for each of the following groups; what general pressure is felt by

    (a) teenagers   (b) parents   (c) old people   (d) everyone?

Then, on your own or in groups, plan a play which looks at *one* of these pressures, and different ways in which it affects different people.

© Paul Francis 1984

First published 1984 by
Edward Arnold (Publishers) Ltd
41 Bedford Square
London WC1B 3DQ

Reprinted 1985

British Library Cataloguing in Publication Data

Francis, Paul
  Under pressure.
  I. Title
  822'.914   PR6057.R/

ISBN 0-7131-0819-3

Phototypeset by The Castlefield Press,
Moulton, Northampton.
Printed in Great Britain, by the Camelot Press, Southampton.